THE BLASPHEMER

THE BLASPHEMER

THE PRICE I PAID FOR REJECTING ISLAM

WALEED AL-HUSSEINI

Arcade Publishing · New York

First published in France as *Blaspémateur*, 2015
First Arcade edition 2017

© Editions Grasset & Fasquelle, 2015

Arcade Publishing books may be purchased in bulk at special discounts for sales promotion, corporate gifts, fund-raising, or educational purposes. Special editions can also be created to specifications. For details, contact the Special Sales Department, Arcade Publishing, 307 West 36th Street, 11th Floor, New York, NY 10018 or arcade@skyhorsepublishing.com.

Arcade Publishing® is a registered trademark of Skyhorse Publishing, Inc.®, a Delaware corporation.

Visit our website at www.arcadepub.com.

10 9 8 7 6 5 4 3 2 1

Library of Congress Cataloging-in-Publication Data is available on file.

Cover design by Erin Seaward-Hiatt

Print ISBN: 978-1-62872-675-6
Ebook ISBN: 978-1-62872-674-9

Printed in the United States of America

Table of Contents

Preface

In this book that tells my story, I would have liked to write more about my parents and my family and describe them as they are: people of modest means, peaceful, loving, and calm. My father worked, as he still does, so that his family could live with dignity. He always wanted his children to attend university, to have a better future. My brothers and sisters persevere in their studies, knowing my parents' hopes for them and what they sacrificed for those hopes to come true. This is my family, for whom I have caused so much suffering and who has always supported me. They are my greatest pride.

Today, it is my turn to protect them and to spare them any further pain by avoiding more conflict with those who would oppose me in my fight. In Palestinian society, any citizen who dares to uphold the freedoms of speech and of religion runs serious dangers, and their families live under constant threat from both their fellow Palestinians and the Palestinian Authority. My father, mother, brothers, and sisters have had to endure disparaging remarks from their own relatives, cutting comments from neighbors, and withering looks from practically everyone else. Ever since I left my homeland in the pursuit of Truth and Freedom, I have become, in the eyes of all these people, a "stain" and a "dishonor," to be washed clean at my family's expense.

Obscurantism is on the rise in Palestinian society, and I continue to be threatened both directly and indirectly through my family. For this reason, I have chosen to keep any mention of my private life and my relations with my family to a strict minimum.

Introduction
Letter to My Brothers

I have never felt hostility toward Muslims. They are all my brothers in humanity. However, the collapse of our societies drives me to despair, and religion is in large part responsible. I respect those who believe, but I despise with all my being their leaders and the ideology that they preach.

If you ask imams why Muslim societies are in such a catastrophic state, they will respond with their usual cynicism: the reason is that we have "left the path of Allah and Islam."

Dear brothers in faith, you would do better to rely on your own intelligence rather than listen to the ready-made arguments of these imams. If what you seek is indeed truth and integrity, if you refuse to content yourselves with texts chosen to shore up unproven tenets of belief, you will never be satisfied with their answers.

My Muslim brothers, I know that you face an existential crisis. Religious leaders are pulling the wool over your eyes with their slogan: "Islam is peace, forgiveness and charity." Nothing could be further from the truth. Islam is the religion of war, battles, massacres, and jihad waged against unbelievers. The Quran tells the faithful to spread the word of Allah around the world, and history, which is rife with conquests and forced adherence to Islam, is proof of the results.

They lull you into submission by telling you that Allah "created you as nations and tribes so you would come to know one another" and fool you by proclaiming: "There are those who believe and those who deny." The truth is that the impure are executed, atheists are persecuted, and Jews and Christians are hounded.

They will tell you that Islam liberated women and put them on equal footing with men. Yet they uphold polygamy, authorize corporal punishment of women, refuse to admit women's testimony in court, and have deprived women of their inheritance rights. As far as they are concerned, our mothers, sisters, and wives belong in Hell.

In contrast to the steady progression and modernization of the rest of the world, Muslims are on a regressive path. Their imams hold them back in order to rebuild the Caliphate. Their goal: to return to the raids and sectarianism of tribal life.

Under Islam, basic human rights and precepts are trampled. The principle of religious freedom for Muslims prevents others from exercising their faith. The equality they profess excludes women and other religions. For them, history began with the Prophet, and everything that preceded him is nonsense.

Yes, my brothers in humanity, I understand your dilemma. But are you for equality and justice or not? Do you believe in basic human rights? Do you respect others? Do you want to live in peace with your neighbors? Will you oppose violence and promote dialogue? You have probably already asked yourselves these questions. Often, however, too often, Muslims give a lukewarm response: they want freedom, aspire to equality, and pledge allegiance to human rights . . . but only if these do not run afoul of Islam.

This book is the story of my experiences and explains my thinking. I hope it will help my Muslim brothers to think for themselves, to fight obscurantism with rational intelligence. My wish is that it will help free them from this sinister religious relic. Will it also inspire non-Muslims to recognize the danger Islam poses for secular societies? Will it encourage them to pay attention to what is happening in the Muslim world today to better protect themselves against it? I sincerely hope so.

There is one thing of which I am sure: whoever reads this book will finish it reassured that, whether they live in a poor neighborhood in a large European city or an entire country where Islam holds sway, they are not alone. They will find in these pages a little more courage to call themselves ex-Muslims.

Waleed al-Husseini

Chapter 1
The Roots of Indignation

Early Childhood

I was born and raised in Qalqilya in the West Bank. My family is Muslim, conservative, and pious, but moderately so. In the Palestine where I grew up, religion was not a choice and still is not. By an inescapable logic, a child inherits both a name and a religion at birth. I became a Muslim by tradition and by education, not by choice. For my parents, who were hardly extremists, Islam was the greatest of all religions: a glorious faith that could "work miracles," "grow minds," and "open hearts," among other magical formulas I heard at home.

For my mother and father, Islam, like sexuality, was a line drawn in the sand. Crossing it was absolutely taboo. They respected the customs of their faith and passed down, first to me, the eldest son, and then to my five sisters and two little brothers, the traditional education that had also been theirs. Like all Muslim families, they applied to the letter the teachings of the Prophet so that his words might come true: "On the Day of Judgement, I will be proud of your multitude before the nations."

Like most young men of my generation, my brothers and I were not burdened by religious obligations. In the traditional Muslim family, the father works and the mother stays home. Even very young boys are free to play and roam at liberty outside the home, but girls are kept inside to perform household chores. Few girls go to school, and those who seek work generally become either teachers in schools for girls or nurses. Men and women are not allowed to have any contact in this society, and the role of women is primarily to bear children and satisfy their husbands' sexual desires. As the first-born son, I was consulted on family matters and generally placed on a higher pedestal than my brothers and sisters. This gave me the freedom to participate in discussions on sensitive matters, transgress certain rules, develop a hunger for the truth, and forge my own personality. It also led me to break many prohibitions and bans.

Nevertheless, my relationship with my mother was especially close. As my educator, advisor, teacher, and confidante, she taught me the values I live by: compassion, kindness, and love for others. As I grew older, however, I realized that Islamic law, at least as it was taught to me and still practiced today, contradicted those same values and prevented a person of faith to reflect, question, and open his mind. How can Islam proclaim that woman is man's inferior while placing on her shoulders the heavy responsibility of raising a family and educating future generations?

School Years

My early childhood was like that of most Palestinians of my generation. For our safety, my friends in Qalqilya and I were not allowed to play outside. We had to find ways to occupy ourselves indoors, in one of our families' homes. But once I began primary school, I discovered a whole new world. I was the top student in my class through my primary and middle school years. I became friends with children from different backgrounds, and my mother was no longer the center of my world. During all those years, however, she was always there to listen to me and guide me through all of my questions and doubts.

It was in high school that I discovered the basic notions of philosophy and Islamic culture. My questions and doubts only multiplied as it became clear to me that the teachings of Islam were impossible to follow in everyday life. Do the faithful exercise free choice or are their actions determined by divine will? This existential question tugged at me constantly. Islam's answer is that man is directed in his decisions and master of them at the same time! My Islamic sciences teacher had no better explanation, telling me that we are at liberty to decide for ourselves in matters we can see and understand, but in those we cannot, our actions are dictated. When I pressed him to explain further, he ordered the adolescent that I was to pray for forgiveness for having blasphemed.

Black-Out

It soon became clear to me that no one—neither at home nor at school and even less at the mosque—could help me with my questions. I began to spend hours at the public library and on the Internet. There I discovered the Mutazilis, who also sought the truth, although without great success. I learned that, although they never tried to spread their ideas, they were considered renegades and apostates and were persecuted. I turned next to the writings of the Ikhwan al-Safa, Sufis, and Wahhabis. I quickly understood that these different theological currents and schools were no more than ill-intentioned groups each trying to steal followers away from the others, throwing curses and fatwas in all directions. They promised Paradise to their followers, but only after enduring the life of hell they imposed.

The more I read, the more questions I had. Why do we know so little about Muslim history? Why are the Muslim philosophers and thinkers and the Mutazilis not taught at Quranic schools or at the mosque?

Hoping to find some answers, I immersed myself in the Quran, the interpretations of Ibn Kathir and Al-Tabari, and the hadiths of Sahih al-Bukhari and Sahih Muslim. To my surprise, I discovered an incalculable number of aberrations and verses espousing ideas contrary to human values, as well as stories of unjust wars and conquests that these texts tried vainly to justify. I found an explanation in the writings of the genealogist Abu Muhammad Abd al-Malik Ibn Hisham, who said Muslims were no better than bandits and their famous conquests were simply raids led in the name of religion. I began to think that the only accomplishment of Islam was to have managed to unite and federate its disciples under the Islamic Nation, or Ummah. To its early warriors, Islam promised the worldly goods and women of the peoples they captured and Paradise to its fallen martyrs. This double-edged promise was the principal motivation behind what are known as the Muslim conquests. I also came to see that the wars of succession after the deaths of the Prophet and the Caliph Ali had little to do with either religion or dogma. These fratricidal wars were waged simply to seize power, according to the dictates of the tribal laws that reigned in the vast Arabian desert, and Islam served to justify the unjustifiable! On the topic of aberrations, however, my greatest surprise came when I discovered how the Prophet's disciples and descendants explained away his unbridled sex life as a way of pardoning his excesses, so that they could enjoy the same practices.

So absurd and self-perpetuating were the "official" texts that I turned next to intellectuals, poets, and writers: the pillars of the literary, cultural, and scientific renaissance in Muslim thought. There again, I was confronted with the fact that all of their views were judged impious, they were persecuted or killed, and their writings were burned.

What was the reason for this iron curtain drawn over Muslim history? Can a religion be thoroughly understood if its past is obscured? Islam has become impervious to the outside and impenetrable for the general public and the majority of its faithful, by masking some essential facts. Are we ever taught that it was the clerics who burned the works of the philosopher Ibn Rushd (Averroës)? Or that the scientist Ibn Sina (Avicenna) was called "the imam of the impure" because his research in philosophy, science, astronomy, and chemistry contradicted the teachings of Islam? Where do we ever learn that the physician Muhammad ibn Zakariyya al-Razi thumbed his nose at clerics and never shied from his apostasy? Or that the translator and thinker Abd Allah Ibn al-Muqaffa was executed at the age of thirty-five for allegedly having offended Islam? Does anyone tell us that Islam's greatest thinkers, including the Imam Al-Shafii, the founder of the Shafii school of Islamic law, decreed that natural science, chemistry, and philosophy were all taboo subjects? Or that still other thinkers authorized the assassinations of scientists whose work might have helped other Muslims think critically about Islam's teachings? The Quran's most famous historian and exegete, Muhammad ibn Jarir al-Tabari, was stoned to death by members of the Hanbali school of orthodox Sunni Islam on charges of apostasy, but this is hushed up, too. No, the true history of Islam was never discussed at school, at home or at the mosque.

Just as in the earliest days of Islam, contemporary history offers still more examples of Muslim intellectuals, thinkers, and scientists persecuted for their beliefs. The Egyptian intellectual Farag Foda was assassinated. The Egyptian theologian Nasr Abu Zayd was forced into exile. Taha Hussein, a pillar of 20th century Arab literature, was taken to task for having published a book on the Jahiliyyah and having criticized Islam. Naguib Mafouz was stabbed for his supposedly "blasphemous" writings. All these endured the same treatment reserved for Abu Nasr al-Farabi, Ibn Rushd, Asphahani, Razi, Ibn Sina, Ghazali, and so many other defenders of the right to think for oneself.

Important authors like these are taught in school, but they are presented as good Muslims. Here lies the hypocrisy of both our current worldly leaders and our educational systems. Although these never call into question the importance of our great writers, they conceal the extent of their thinking and the persecutions they endured. All were hunted down, assassinated, hung, or poisoned in the name of Islam. Why do we never learn this? Is Islam so fragile that it might crumble under the slightest criticism? Could God himself be afraid of words and debate?

As children, we are taught that the mysteries of life are known to God alone and that critical thinking is forbidden. For religious leaders, individual opinions are *haram*: proscribed by Islamic law. According to this principle, understanding religion, God, and the prophets is completely taboo. Obscurantism has cast a deep shadow over Muslim societies but shores up religion and allows it to propagate without fear of reprisal. To hold sway over the faithful, leaders have a powerful pill, administered five times daily, at the precise moment of the muezzin's call to prayer. As soon as it rings out, people come running to the mosque and bow their heads to the ground in a sign of submission. Before the pill wears off, their minds, already fogged by religion, are subjected to a fresh injection of preaching. The ecstasy they experience in this state puts their critical capacities to sleep and, in their place, awakens the supernatural realms promised by their religious leaders, far from the realities of truth, materiality, and reason. Etherized, the faithful live under an illusion, allowing matters of their own existence to be decided for them by their religious leaders who pretend to be God's representatives on earth and who claim to speak in his name.

These leaders have convinced us that we are no better than a herd of animals who must follow them. They have conditioned us into subservience, and we have withdrawn into ourselves. They have taught us to be afraid of others and the unknown. They have engraved in our minds that we must bow to the accepted wisdom of the group and never think for ourselves, as this could lead us away from the Ummah, Islam, and God's will. For them, life is inextricably linked to religion, which makes the rules by which we live. The culture they have promoted is exploitative of others, bigoted toward non-Muslims, and oppresses women, who are considered inferior beings culturally, spiritually, and physically: mere flesh to be disposed of at their masters' whims. They have legitimized religious interference in people's private lives, imposing a lifestyle, spiritual beliefs, and religious practice.

Employing both the carrot and the stick (where the carrot is Heaven and the stick Hell), religious leaders have deprived us of our most basic rights. Brandishing sharia law and *Sunnah* (the teachings of Muhammad), they have drawn Muslims away from research, science, exploration, and reflection and have brainwashed generation after generation, depriving them of freedom, dignity, humanity, progress, and a future.

The so-called revolutionaries and rebels—those who have managed to escape this brainwashing—are simply rational individuals who want to reflect on, understand, and explore life and the value of a human life. Through my research and reading and by exercising my own intelligence, I was able to join this informal club of free men.

A Short-Lived Respite

For two years in high school, I endured the brainwashing administered by my religious teachers. Alone in my intellectual crisis, I no longer felt confident broaching questions with my friends and family, even those closest to me, not even my mother and confidante. As momentous as this physical and spiritual upheaval was, it was nothing compared to what I would undergo later and that would forever change my life. However, It was enough to convince me that Islam is not a divine religion, that the Quran is not a holy text, and that Muhammad was neither a Prophet nor a messenger of God. I was still an adolescent, moreover one firmly indoctrinated by Islam. To begin to look differently at my world—to consider the fallibility of imams or read the Quran as an ordinary book, open to discussion and criticism—was no simple task. I was emboldened by my convictions, however, and I knew that I had to find an outlet for them if I ever hoped to be at peace with myself.

I threw myself into studying for my final exams to graduate from high school. This was one way to calm my mind and chase away the intellectual fog I was in. The experience was like a second birth for me, and I passed with high marks. Although I no longer considered myself a Muslim, I received the highest grade of my graduating class—a near perfect 96/100—in Islamic Culture, the subject that is the most heavily weighted in the final calculation of students' overall grades. The irony of this did not escape me.

In the West Bank, however, Islam is a required course for Muslims and non-Muslims both, from their earliest days at school. This means that, whatever their religion, whether they are Muslim, Catholic, or Jewish, Palestinian children are immersed in the violence of the Quran. At the very least, to discourage new suicide bombers, these youngest of students deserve to be provided clear explanations of texts calling for Muslims to kill all non-Muslims. The opposite is true, however; the educational system does not shrink in the least from training whole generations of radical Islamists. Is there any justification for this kind of mass brainwashing of children, fed at the breast of hate and violence, no matter what their own religious beliefs might be? Or isn't this a valid question to be asking?

If I decry the sheer madness and rage that threatens children educated in this way, it is to send a wake-up call to save innocent children from learning at school and at prayers to become criminals. Because, make no mistake about it, in my country and throughout the Muslim world, the main exporters of terrorists are the mosques.

University Years

With my high school diploma under my belt, I enrolled at the Arab American University of Jenin. Studying information technology and computer administration, I quickly discovered the vast possibilities and uses of the Internet. I was "areligious," of course, but I lacked the courage to fully assume my new convictions, much less make them public. My personal search for the truth continued, but I didn't dare ask myself whether I believed in God anymore: I was still a prisoner of my religious education. I had always prayed to God to help me with whatever life posed as a challenge or a wish: good grades in school or a new bike for my birthday. If God didn't exist, to whom could I turn for help? How would I pass my exams the next time? Had my prayers been in vain? Was I crazy? I avoided reading anything that questioned the existence of God in those years: my earlier struggle with the question had been too futile and painful to relive. I felt isolated from society, but the Muslim environment of my upbringing kept me from going over the edge.

Then, one day, I found the courage to take the bull by the horns. I began to widen my reading, starting with philosophical and scientific works that proposed to examine the question of God, such as *The God Delusion* by Richard Dawkins. Here, I finally found the answers that religion alone had not been able to provide. Diving into the works of Darwin, Stephen Hawking, and other scientists who left their mark on humanity, I discovered that the majority of them were atheists. I also began to understand why they had never made it into the curricula of our schools and universities: quite simply, Dawkins's work and Darwin's Theory of Natural Selection are antithetical to the primacy of religion over science in the Muslim world.

My plunge into Western civilization and thought caused me to break many taboos. Thanks to the Internet, which opened the door to entirely new horizons, I learned about the whole vast evolution of humanity.

Tearing out the bars that had enclosed me in the cage of my Oriental culture, I multiplied the stores of my intellectual and scientific knowledge and completely changed my outlook on the world. On the Internet, I also learned that the famed miracles of Islam, invoked by our religious leaders and faithfully repeated by both print media and Islamic satellite television, were only lies.

The Arab world is full of preachers who exercise a form of intellectual terrorism, facilitated by the fact that the population at large has no means of calling into question the authenticity of their so-called knowledge. Challenging an imam is akin to violating a sacred oath. The infallibility of religious leaders always was and still remains a central problem for Muslim cultures. Another major problem is that Islam not only purports to be the arbiter of the relationship between the individual and his Creator; under Islam, divine law dictates all aspects of daily life, even the most intimate ones. Rejecting those laws is therefore all the more difficult: throwing off Islam is the same as abandoning a whole way of being.

As I pursued my reading of Western thinkers, I, too, feared losing my moral compass but soon learned that precious new tools of thinking and reflection were now at my disposal. Darwin's theory of evolution was wholly more convincing than the story of the Garden of Eden. How could anyone ever accept the idea that God encouraged the descendants of Adam and Eve to be fruitful and multiply amongst themselves when all religions, and none less emphatically than Islam, condemn incest? Doesn't logic demand that God would have created more than one Adam and more than one Eve so that their children could have avoided marrying each other, in violation of the laws later instituted by their self-appointed heirs? The story is silent on this point.

For six months, I suffered through rationalizations like these, challenging myself to reject everything I had been taught and had believed until then. If God was my guide and my support, I was surely lost. Was there any meaning to my life? Where could I turn for protection when I most needed it? To whom could I pray? The realization that I could no longer rely on God as my help and savior and that there was no difference between invoking a divine power and a stone was intolerable to me.

Once I had abandoned my illusions, however, I set myself new objectives and began looking for ways to find meaning in my life. I joined online forums and became familiar with the websites of certain Muslim preachers and imams. Using different pseudonyms, I opened a dozen accounts on a website for atheist Arabs, which quickly became the target of Islamists who used it to post insults and publish fatwas. My usernames identified me variously as either an atheist, an Islamist, a doubter, or as having no religious affiliation at all, my idea being to launch a debate that would weaken the positions of the preachers on the site. At times, I even debated with myself, using my different pseudonyms, in the hope of encouraging other Internet users to join the discussion. I needed reassurance that there were others out there like me who were doubting, questioning, and searching for answers. The ones who were the most vocal, however, were the administrators of the religious websites, and their rhetoric only strengthened my convictions.

My Divorce from Islam . . .

It took me six years to finally leave Islam and consider myself a nonbeliever. I had no idea how to tell people, however, much less call myself an atheist and live my life accordingly. How would all my friends, my family, and my acquaintances take the news? Beyond my personal circles, what other repercussions could there be for me? Should I make a public announcement, and how? I was overwhelmed by questions.

Convinced that the university was the most open place I knew and that my fellow students were the most likely to understand my decision, I decided to begin by telling my friends, most of whom primarily spent their time at torrid parties where all kinds of alcohol and even drugs were freely available. They of all people would accept my new identity and support me, I reasoned. It was at one of these parties, held far off campus, that I announced to everyone there that I no longer believed in the Prophet, in Islam, or in the existence of God. It was a very warm night and there were drinks and girls in abundance, yet my declaration hit the party like a cold shower. In the deathly silence that ensued, one of the guests spoke up:

"Waleed, you're drunk. Stop drinking." I said I wasn't drunk and repeated what I had said. You could have heard a pin drop. I was terrified, frozen in place by the daggers in everyone's eyes. The party quickly broke up, and I spent the rest of the night besieged by anxiety and doubt. Should I have shut my mouth? Pretended to recant? Out of the question, I told myself: I was not going to lie to my friends anymore, no matter how afraid I was.

There was a general climate of fear and insecurity in the West Bank at that time. Weapons were readily accessible, and the Islamists could have gunned me down at any moment. Every day saw a new conflict between different armed groups, Hamas and Fatah, Islamic Jihad and the Popular Resistance Committees, or between rival families or two hostile organizations. Walking in the street could be a matter of life or death, bringing you under a shower of bullets or into the battlefield of warring factions. How many innocent people died because someone falsely accused them of being Israeli agents? How many bystanders paid with their lives for some group's vendetta?

This chaos was the fault of the Palestinian Authority. Palestinians had hoped the powers in place would usher in a breed of governance unlike anything else in the Arab world. Collective and individual freedoms, including the freedom of speech, would be protected; human rights, pluralism, and diversity would be respected; and the rule of law would finally be applied. Our disappointment was all the more crushing. The Palestinian Authority simply continued down the path of existing Arab regimes, revoking basic freedoms, imprisoning hundreds of opponents, shutting down the offices of political parties, and banning the independent media. Even the progovernment newspapers were censored, and some issues were removed from newsstands for having tested the limits of what was allowed. With so many partisan factions, finding employment in the civil service and security sectors required meeting draconian criteria. The rare services and aid offered by the government were also reserved for carefully selected beneficiaries sharing the reigning ideological and political sensibilities.

Fed by such disorder, chaos grew like weeds. Criminals acted with total impunity, knowing they would never be brought to justice, while their victims were doubly sentenced, bearing the full brunt of this lawlessness. The West Bank became a huge jungle where only might made right. In Zababdeh, where I was living as a student, arms were ever more accessible to the general public and circulated freely. The official explanation was that weapons were needed to fight enemy groups, but, in reality, they were used to settle scores among civilians.

Some unavoidable conclusions had to be drawn from the fateful night of my announcement: the topic of religion is a line that can never be crossed; Islam refuses all criticism, even from those who ignore its teachings; it is impossible to wean individuals from their religious convictions, having been fed these since infancy; society would spurn me. I became convinced that religion is an obstacle to all human relations. I steeled myself to face the inevitable situation that loomed before me.

. . . and What Came of It

The next day, and over the days that followed, no one said a single word to me. Alone or in groups, they avoided me, preferring to whisper behind my back. The news that I was an atheist spread like wildfire to the entire student body at the university, where I began to hear myself called a *kafir* (nonbeliever), among other insults and forms of verbal aggression. They never tried to harm me, though, and I never reported any of my tormentors to the university. That would have been riskier by far!

Rejected as I was by everyone at the university, my friends first and foremost, the only people who approached me either came to ask me questions or make fun of the madman I had become in their eyes. They taunted me, using Islam's usual arguments, whose absurdity was unsettling. I did, however, have a close female friend who, though not an atheist, had become a skeptic. She hadn't come to her decision through the kind of research I had done, but she shared my views. We spent a great deal of time together, but we were careful to steer our conversations to more general topics rather than dogma. Nevertheless, I had difficulty adjusting to my forced isolation; the generally hurtful ambiance was unbearable to me. I had to accept that ostracism is the fate of non-Muslims and resolve to make the best of it.

I held out until the end of my second semester. I refused to consider abandoning either my studies or, worse, my friend. In the West Bank, as in most Arab-speaking countries, the only place where men and women are allowed to interact is at university. Outside of that context, religion forbids it, which only heightens the sense of frustration, leading to harassment and rape. Religion is the main cause of the problems of Muslim youth.

Because of her friendship with me, my friend was hounded at the university and in her residency hall. The other women with whom she lived interrogated her relentlessly about our relationship and about me. They even demanded to know if she was still a virgin and threatened to examine her themselves to settle the question, even though they had boyfriends of their own while hiding behind their veils and their apparent religious convictions. In the society in which I was raised, sex is a crime, however everyone is obsessed with it. If a young woman is known to frequent a certain young man, she becomes a pariah, a "whore" who can be executed without trial, to wash her family's honor. Meanwhile, no law exists to punish the perpetrators of her so-called "honor" killing.

In the patriarchal societies of the Middle East, man is an oppressor both at home and in public. Women are thought to be physically and intellectually inferior; in the eyes of religion, they are incomplete, and their opinion has no weight. Man is the master of all, and when he punishes his women, he demonstrates his supreme wisdom. A woman can therefore be judged guilty of a crime, condemned to die, and executed, and no man will raise his voice to defend her, whereas only admiration is bestowed on her killer.

By associating with me, my female friend was in danger of being judged impious and worse; hemmed in by privations and obsessed with sex, the pious systematically take advantage of girls with more liberated ideas because they are the easiest sexual targets.

At the end of our second semester, my friend's family decided she should transfer to a different university. Friends had alerted them to the atmosphere on campus, which made them fear for their daughter's safety. Her parents were progressive liberals and civil rights activists who were known for their tolerance, moderation, and openness, but their allowing her to live on her own as a student, far from her family and friends in another city, had raised eyebrows; it was highly unusual. After she left, I felt more alone than ever and in danger of falling into a deep depression.

After thinking long and hard about what to do, I finally decided it was time for me, as well, to transfer to another university, where I would never share my opinions with anyone. I told myself that my priority was to get my degree and earn a living. I had no desire to ruin my chances in life, and even less to get myself killed. I moved to Jerusalem, where I felt much safer. I managed to make friends by hiding my atheism from them, although I didn't say daily prayers, go to the mosque, or fast during Ramadan. I pleaded laziness at first, but eventually my double life was too much for me. I finally confided in my mother, who was an assiduous reader of the Quran and other sacred texts, as well as interpretations of these. Her faith came naturally to her, unfettered by doubt.

My intention was never to enter into a debate with her, and even less to convince her to renounce her religion; I just needed to unburden myself of a suffocating weight. The day I told her that I had become an atheist, she said that she wasn't surprised and that she had been praying daily that God might enlighten me and put me back on the path of Islam. Nevertheless, she didn't disown me. The power of my mother's love for me brought me some peace and helped me focus on my studies.

Cyberspace was my refuge, as it is for many former Muslims. Young men of my generation mostly used the Web to visit porn sites or go on forums to meet girls, something they could never do in broad daylight. They also played video games, one of the few distractions possible under the curfew. But that was the extent of what was available to them for amusement.

It was about the same time that I began blogging.

Chapter II
Rebellious Writings

A Personal Journey

I created a Facebook page and plunged into the fascinating world of social media. However, I couldn't find a single site or a single group criticizing Islam or discussing atheism. I gathered that Muslim youths weren't interested in either. So, one night, with just a few clicks, I created an atheist group of my own. I thought of myself as a veritable pioneer.

I posted short texts, questioning the existence of God or asking others to comment on Islamic law or passages from the Quran. I soon learned that my former fellow Muslims were not very well informed about their religion. To defend it, they cut and pasted the arguments of various ulemas, without either understanding those arguments or even seeming to have read them.

Through a hundred different ruses, I did manage to discover that many other people were struggling with the same questions as I was, though they typically abandoned them out of fear of ending up in Hell.

Legitimate Cause

My main reason for creating my own space on the Internet was to let off some steam, but it wasn't long before blogging became a necessity for me.

I felt an obligation to help people who were asking questions in vain; I wanted them to benefit from my years of research to find the answers that could help them. But unlike the ulemas, I didn't pretend I knew what the truth was. I took this as my approach and translated it into a forum and a blog called "The Voice of Reason" (Noor al-Aqel - نودون رون العقل). I was seventeen at the time. Not only was this the first Arab-language blog dedicated to atheism and a critique of religion, but it was also a forerunner for a new way of thinking in the Arab world.

Toward the end of 2006, I expanded the content of the blog, which began to treat philosophical and existential questions as much as Islam or the Quran's so-called scientifically proven miracles. The hundred or so entries I posted on these topics were read by 1 million people. According to Google and Wikipedia, "The Voice of Reason" was getting over seventy thousand hits every week, until access to it was blocked by several Islamist and Arab countries, beginning with Saudi Arabia and followed by the other Gulf states and Tunisia.

In the early days, visitors to the site mostly came to insult me, call me a traitor to Islam, and threaten to take down the site. Beginning in 2007, however, the posts took a more positive tone, and the beginnings of a dialogue started to take root. I was proud to think I had been the one to create this ripple and to see how, over time, it had become a wave of almost tsunami proportions washing over the Middle East and North Africa. The number of proclaimed atheists exploded, and many more sites appeared. More than 80 blogs were created in different countries to spread my ideas; every one of them invited me to be its administrator.

The topics of discussion widened again. Is it necessary to fast during Ramadan? Should religious affiliation appear on ID cards? Some wondered why the facts of the Prophet's life had been airbrushed. Others made fun of ulemas who preach on satellite television. Still others employed logic and science to point out Islam's contradictions. And certain sites, at last, denounced the humiliating status of women. All of these blogs found their inspiration in "The Voice of Reason," whose popularity had exploded.

Some Philosophical Questions

The first question I posted was the one that had worried me so much as a child: does man have free will? By way of an answer, an imam made a fool of himself by proposing the following story.

One day, the imam offered his son a choice between a chocolate bar and a cement block, knowing full well that his son would choose the chocolate. Precisely, he wrote on the blog, the child chose the chocolate. Did that mean the imam forced him to choose it? According to his reasoning, God knew that the boy would choose the chocolate bar. From that, the imam concluded that man submits to God's will, rather than exercise his own, and that, by the same logic, God knew even before I was born that I, Waleed al-Husseini, would go to Hell. Seen from a different angle, however, other solutions become apparent:

- On the one hand, if I have free will, it lies in my power to prove God's prediction for me wrong and go to Heaven. However, if I can prove God wrong, God is neither omnipotent nor omniscient.
- On the other hand, if, no matter what I do, I have to submit to what God has willed for me and go to Hell, then God is evil because he predestined me to burn in the eternal fires. This also means that God is not filled with the goodness that the ulemas say he is, because he made his own choice to punish me without ever considering my actions and whether I deserved this punishment. If God is not good, then neither does he have any of the positive qualities, such as mercy, that are attributed to him. If God is unjust and unkind, then he isn't God.
- It follows that there is no middle ground: either God cannot know in advance what choices I will make, or he is unjust and unkind by making me choose the path of evil, to punish me. In both cases, the contradictions are obvious and radically undermine the divinity and the superiority of God.

On my blog, I also raised the question of the creation of the world. Why did God create man? What did he stand to benefit? Only two logical solutions exist: either God created man because he needed him or God didn't need humans but created them anyway. What other possibility can there be?

However, if God needed man and created him to fill that need, he cannot be perfect. In school, we learn that God is perfect and superior and has no need of us, but the argument that says that God does not need man, yet created him anyway, is an insult to God, who appears so flippant and extravagant that he created something he doesn't need. Back in the real world, if I decided to build a car or a computer, it would mean that I had a real need and use for these. If not, I would be wasting my time. But since our religious leaders insist that God doesn't need us, the logical conclusion is that God's decision to create something for which he doesn't have any need at all is an utterly incoherent decision. If God is fickle and capricious, as this choice would demonstrate he is, then he can no longer be described as perfect and divine.

On the question of the existence of God, some Muslims argue that the human mind is unable to ponder such a profound concept. Yet God also orders us to seek the truth. Wouldn't this so-called "perfect" God have made a mistake by asking us to do this with our limited minds? These examples prove our Creator to be either imperfect or cruel, since his crea-tion—man—is deliberately flawed.

Suppose I invented a computer with 160 gigabytes of memory, even though I might have designed it to have 500 gigabytes. Either the 160 gigabyte computer is the best I could do, or I deliberately made an infe-rior product, in which case I'm at fault, which is also to say I am human.

In Surah At-Tin (95) of the Quran, the Prophet says, "We created man of the best stature." It stands to reason to conclude that God could not have done better than he did when he made man. A defective creation can only come from a defective creator.

Another subject that provoked intense debate had to do with the natural laws that Muslims consider to be divinely ordered. The Muslim faithful believe that all the known laws of both nature and physics were created by God, yet they never ask themselves, "Who created God?" That would put the one who created those laws and those who enjoy their benefits on equal footing.

At first, their argument seems admissible, but it does not hold up to close reading of what is recorded on this topic in various sacred texts. The argument goes that the laws of physics apply to God, meaning they predate him. But that would mean that some other force must have created the laws, and then God. The Prophet says in the Quran, "Your Lord is Allah, who created the heavens and the earth in six days and then mounted the throne of power" (Surah Al-Araf 54). The Prophet recognizes the existence of a throne, in other words, a chair or seat, adding, "His throne (*kursi*) extends over the heavens and the earth" (Surah Al-Baqarah 255). Here, Muhammad describes God resting on a throne after having created the earth, the heavens, and man. What intrigues me here is the fact that God is resting.

If God is truly omnipotent and exempt from the laws of nature, why would he need to rest in a chair? Furthermore, by sitting in a chair, he is proving himself subject to the force of gravity. Not content with a single contradiction, the Quran mentions the throne again, but this time it rests on water: "And it is He who created the heavens and the earth in six days, and His throne had been upon water" (Surah Hud 11). Water is a natural element found on several planets, including the Earth. Muhammad is clearly saying that God's throne floats on water and that God sits in it. Muhammad therefore believes that water and gravity exist in heaven. Muslims will simply retort that there is no contradiction between believing that God is seated on a throne and not knowing how this is possible. They will also say that it is an error to compare God to other creatures: Muhammad said: "There is nothing like Him" (Surah Ash-Shura 11). However, in that case, how is it possible to believe that a natural element like water and a natural phenomenon like gravity can have any bearing on God, who is supernatural? The contradictions in this reasoning are glaring.

We discussed other religions, as well, and compared other legends to our own. One example we used was that of Ganesh, the son of Shiva and

Parvati. According to legend, Ganesh was born with a human head while his father was on a military campaign. When Ganesh was five years old, he was standing watch at the door while his mother, Parvati, was bathing. Shiva appeared suddenly, having just returned from the war, but he didn't notice his son. Ganesh, following his mother's orders, forbade his father from entering the room. Furious at this impertinence from a child, Shiva cut off his head. Parvati asked him to restore her son, so he ordered his men to bring him the head of the first living creature they found. This is how Ganesh got his elephant's head.

This story can seem as ridiculous as the one that Muslims cherish in which an angel with six hundred wings blew over a virgin so that she would conceive. In reality, these are mere legends, and they must be understood as such.

Every religion is founded on a god who punishes and disciplines his disciples by releasing the forces of the natural world, whether as eruptions, earthquakes, or tsunamis . . . These kinds of natural disasters affect everyone, however: Buddhists, Jews, Hindus, and Christians, as well as Muslims. Why then do we say that earthquakes kill the Japanese unbelievers, that tsumanis devastate Muslim Indonesia, that hurricanes destroy Christian churches in the United States, or that famine attacks animists in Africa or Muslims in Somalia? The single common denominator here is the way these catastrophes are interpreted: the faithful assume that they are the victims of divine vengeance. Could God be so evil that he would willingly punish and kill his own creatures?

Any reader of the Quran and the Bible will notice immediately that these religions depict their god as a living being who is able to feel both love and hatred. Jews call themselves "God's chosen people." Muslims are proud to be the "best nation created for mankind." Either way, each religion's god seems to cherish his own disciples and detest those of other religions. I was taught as a child that the God of Islam hates Jews and calls on Muslims to fight against them and that this God reserves particular sufferings for Jews in the afterlife. Nevertheless, God's existence has never been proven, despite legends that have been passed down over thousands of years in which God appeared to mortals. If he does exist, is it normal that God sits back and watches his disciples kill one another for hundreds of years in his name? Why didn't he send us a messenger to guide us and save us from our suffering? If he sent us the prophets, the last of whom, presumably, lived 1,400 years ago, why doesn't he send any more to deliver man from his distress? If our ancestors met God and his messengers and if, as they claim, they returned with proof of what they saw, why did they never share this evidence with us? After so much time spent mulling these questions, I finally concluded that religions were created to serve political interests.

I also took note of the fact that God refrains from working miracles on Earth. What other explanation can there be for the goodness God showers on the chosen people of Israel, whereas famine decimates whole populations in Africa? Wouldn't it make more sense for God to turn his attention to Africa to save millions from famine, thirst, and AIDS?

The Quran's Naïveté

Once I had reasoned that far, I began to see the utter naïveté of the stories told in the Quran. I was especially struck by those who pretend to show examples of divine punishment and rewards: the storms and floods and lightening bolts sent to reprimand a rebellious people. Doesn't this way of speaking to the faithful also show a deliberate intention to terrorize them into submission? The Quran never speaks of the people who make it to Paradise. Is it because no one ever took the Prophet at his word and believed in it? It seemed clear to me that the Quran is an arbitrary and illogical text that dangles either a carrot or a stick to help religious leaders better control their flock. Why does God get angry when people disobey him? Isn't he supposed to know already if people are going to refuse to worship him? Isn't anger a human condition, caused by a biochemical reaction in the brain? And why is it that God no longer sends cataclysmic punishments to those who disobey him, as the sacred texts tell us he used to? This last question always dogged me.

Even today, the more I read the Quran, the more convinced I am that atheism is the only reasonable position. Every passage further solidifies my conviction that this book could never be the word of any god. It's impossible that this presumed deity vaunts his power, promising either punishment or rewards; that he loses his temper, insults and prepares his revenge; that he's even happy or sad; that he prays for his messenger and consults the angels; that he inspects Heaven and Hell; that he intervenes in the private affairs of his Prophet; that he authorizes the rape of women, the plunder of his enemies and the murder of dissenters . . . It is inconceivable that God, whatever he may be, could order his Prophet to wage battle against the sinful and the heretics, as if he, the Almighty, weren't able to do it himself. If you take what's written in the Quran at face value, God is by far the worst kind of man there is. Which is why I have concluded that "God" is a pure invention of the Bedouins: a naïve, backward, petty, morally reprehensible, resentful voyeur, a god who slips into a couple's bedroom to watch and listen to everything that goes on there, a god who encourages his disciples to engage in criminal acts, a god who believes the sun sets into the mud of the earth, a god who flies into a rage if his faithful are lax in their worship of him but who is happy if they fast for a day in his name. What kind of a god is that?

The Quran's Distortion of the Scientific Miracle

Muslims can discourse endlessly on the "Scientific Miracle" revealed by the Quran. For years, I was astonished by the anomalies I could identify regarding the science of the so-called sacred texts. This was the main reason for my atheism. For Muslims, the Quran contains discoveries that science has been able to explain only recently. For me, it was apparent from my exchanges with visitors to my blog—renowned ulemas—that they were deliberately lying to me. Yet it was hard to believe that the only way they found to convince me of Islam's truth was by resorting to trickery.

A particularly ridiculous example involves the sun. In the Surah Yasin 38, it is written, "The sun runs its course for a period determined by the Almighty, the All-Knowing." Although there are ulemas who have tried to explain the sun's rising and setting, Muhammad got it all wrong. Sheikh Mohammad Mansour offered the explanation that no one other than the

Almighty could know where the sun set, a conclusion shared by Sayyid Qutb.

In his book *Sahih*, Imam al-Bukhari makes reference to Abu Dharr al-Ghifari, who was a disciple of the Prophet and who tells this story. One day, he was seated next to the Prophet in a mosque. When the sun set, the Prophet asked his disciple if he knew where the sun went. He replied that only God and his messenger knew the answer. The Prophet then said, "The sun goes until it prostrates itself in the hands of the Creator. There it seeks permission to leave and permission is granted to it. It rises again and leaves its house" (Al-Bukhari, *Sahih*, 3199).

In the 1970s, the former mufti of Saudi Arabia, Muhammad ibn al Uthaymeen used this preposterous *hadith* to decree a fatwa on any Muslim claiming that the Earth revolved around the Sun. For him, of course, the opposite was true.

And while scientific evidence has mounted for years against the Quran, ulemas still knowingly teach their lie. How can they? And why do so many Muslims put their faith in these charlatans? Religious leaders have a saying, "The wise man needs only one example to believe but even a thousand examples won't convince a fool." The adage remains true.

The Teachings of Islam

The seventh century saw the establishment of many Islamic laws that reflect a reigning barbarity. These laws were aimed at legitimizing for Muslims the raids, massacres, rapes, destruction, pillage, and oppression that were the rule of the day.

Much can be learned from these ancient laws about Islam's current position on women: she is an inferior being, a mere sexual object presented in the shape of a devil. Man's unequal, she will inherit half as much as her brother, and her testimony in a trial is given half as much weight as a man's. The law condones violence and humiliation used against her but also demands that she submit to the sexual desires of her husband, who may take several wives. If a woman uses perfume, she is considered a prostitute. If she goes out in public without a male chaperone, she can be hung, and she must always be covered by a dehumanizing veil. It is also a precept of Islam that all women go to Hell and that those who escape their fate and make it to Heaven will have to share their husbands with the 72 *houris* that are promised to the faithful there. In other words, the best a woman can hope for from Islam is be a prostitute in Heaven.

Islamic law is full of outrages: thieves have their hands amputated, and any woman who has sexual relations with a man who is not her husband is stoned to death. The cruelest law stipulates that traitors are beheaded. This is the same law that I braved when I decided to leave Islam and declare myself an atheist. Where is the justice in that law, when I never chose to become a Muslim of my own accord? Islam was thrust upon me when I was born; it was only as I grew older that I discovered that I did not agree with this religion and its teachings and decided to leave. How could I be accused of betraying Islam when I never joined it voluntarily? Given the way it treats deserters, Islam looks a lot more like the mafia or an organized crime network than a religion.

Muhammad and Women

According to several historical sources, Muhammad's childhood was simple and austere and far different from the upbringing of his contemporaries. He followed a rule of asceticism that kept women at a certain remove for a good part of his life, contrary to what was the norm at the time. He was twenty-five years old when he married Khadijah, a woman fifteen years his elder, and had his first sexual experience. They were married for twenty-five years, during which Muhammad never took another wife.

Khadijah's death marked the end of that life, however. The Prophet took thirteen wives in the thirteen years following her death, and he lived with eleven of these simultaneously. Only a close study of his psychology can explain such a profound transformation.

In her book on the Prophet's first wife, *Cover Me, Khadijah* (*Ya Khadija Dathirini*, Beirut, Dar Al-Talia, 1999), Salwa Belhaj Saleh al-Ayeb explains the nature of the power Khadijah wielded over Muhammad:

"Khadijah was a rich shopkeeper who asked the indigent orphan Muhammad to marry her . . . Her strong personality and wealth acted as obstacles to Muhammad's even dreaming of taking a second wife. By marrying Khadijah and her riches, Muhammad gained not only a wife but also a very comfortable life. She controlled him completely and refused to share him with another woman."

After Khadijah's death, Muhammad married a much older woman, Sawda bint Zama, but when age began to take its toll on her, he asked for a divorce. She managed to dissuade him by proposing he take a third wife, Aisha, the daughter of Abu Bakr al-Siddiq. Sawda held the power but from behind the scenes.

It is important to remember that Aisha was only six years old when the Prophet married her and only nine when she began to live under his roof and have sexual relations with him, a fifty-two-year old man. Many more wives would follow. It's not hard to conclude that Khadijah's death marked a sexual liberation in Muhammad's private life and that his new-found sexuality was unleashed by his public stature, as a religious, political, and military leader who personally led numerous raids on the enemy. During these, the lion's share of the takings, which naturally included women, went to the commander-in-chief. His wives Safiyah bint Huyay and Juwayriyah bint al-Harith were the spoils of war.

Muhammad led the life of any political and military leader of his day, accumulating marriages and sexual conquests that he legitimized on religious grounds. Today, Muslim traditionalists use various arguments to justify this "bulimic polygamy," insisting that these marriages advanced important political, social, and even religious interests. By encouraging the practice of taking multiple wives, Muhammad also pulled men indirectly into Islam.

Some questions remain, however. If his polygamy was only a form of proselytism to swell the numbers of the faithful, why didn't he practice it as soon as he had his first "revelations" when he was married to Khadijah? At that time, Islam and Muhammad were under significant pressure from outside forces: conflicts that might have been resolved through marriage. In reality, traditionalists deliberately obscure an important fact: all of

Muhammad's wives were beautiful women, for whom the Prophet naturally had a weak spot. The sixth-century Islamic scholar Abu al-Farash Ibn al-Jawzi wrote: "Muhammad married Aisha, who was very beautiful. He saw Zaynab and was seduced by her beauty. He married her. He chose Safiyah for the same reasons. If word came to him that a girl was beautiful, he sent his men to ask for her in marriage" (*Sayd al-Khatir*, 180). Although traditionalist texts would have us believe that his wives were divorced or widowed women whom no man desired, beauty and charm were the principal characteristics of all of his women.

Some of these same texts cite Aisha: "The Prophet married Umm Salama. I was greatly saddened when it was reported to me that she was dazzlingly beautiful. I asked to see her. She was even more beautiful than I had imagined" (Al-Montazem 208/3).

Al-Tabari (232/2) also describes Zaynab bint Jahsh as a very beautiful woman: "One day, Muhammad made his way to the home of Zaynab's husband, Zayd, his protégé, who was absent at the time. The Prophet glimpsed a lightly dressed Zaynab and exclaimed: 'Glory be to the One who speaks to the heart. Zayd has divorced Zaynab so Muhammad could marry her.'" Tafsir al-Qurtubi provides more saucy details in his version of the story: "Muhammad went to see Zayd, who was not at home. He saw Zaynab, a light-skinned woman who was one of the most beautiful in the tribe. He desired her immediately and exclaimed, 'Glory be to the One who speaks to the heart. God has sent a gust of wind to lift Zaynab's robes so that Muhammad might appreciate her beauty.'"

Ibn Ishaq (Al-Sirah: 294/2) also mentions Aisha in his explanation of Muhammad's marriage to the beautiful Juwayriyah bint al-Harith, who was twenty years old at the time. Juwayriyah bint al-Harith became the Prophet's eighth wife, after her capture in the battle of Banu Mustaliq, during which her husband, Mustafa bin Safwan, was killed. She was at first taken captive by a companion of Muhammad, Thabit Ibn Qays. Frightened by her new situation, she sought protection from Muhammad, pleading for mercy. As soon as Aisha saw her, she knew that the younger woman's beauty would sway her husband and hated her instantly. She wasn't wrong: Muhammad offered to free her from Thabit Ibn Qays's captivity by marrying her. As for Hafsah bint Umar, Muhammad threatened her with divorce on several occasions but never followed through for political reasons: her father, Omar, was a powerful dignitary who became the second caliph after Abu Bakr in the years following the Prophet's death.

Muhammad also tried to add Asma bint al-Numan to his list of wives, but a jealous Aisha prevented the marriage. She was afraid that Asma's legendary beauty would distract Muhammad from his existing marital duties (Al-Tabari, in *Al-Samat Al-Thamine*, 126, "The Precious Account of the Virtues of the Mothers of the Believers").

Muhammad's most famous woman by far, however, remains Maria al-Qibtiyya (Maria the Copt), although she was not his wife in marriage but his legal consort. She was one in a long line of women who served to satisfy the Prophet's libido.

Islam's Crimes and Ethnic Cleansing

Muhammad's many marriages are not only proof of his insatiable sexual appetite. They also have much to teach us about the political and military context of his day. One of his wives, Safiyah bint Huyay, was a Jew from the Banu Nadir tribe and taken captive at the Battle of Khaybar. The Muslims' attack on the Banu Nadir, one of the first known crimes against humanity, is difficult to explain: Muhammad had no justifiable reason to declare war on them. According to Muslim texts (though there were no witnesses), the angel Jibril (Gabriel) appeared to the Prophet to reproach him for ceasing the wars of Islamization and to bring him a divine order to wipe out the Jews. This is a convenient explanation for an otherwise unjustifiable and murderous military campaign: how else could the Muslims have declared war in the absence of any existing conflict? But why would a reputedly almighty God even need Muhammad and his men to do his work for him?

When the Battle of Khaybar was declared, Muhammad gave the order to execute every male—children, adults, and the elderly—to capture all the women and girls—who then became slaves—and to pillage the tribe's possessions. To his own warriors, he explained that this cruelty was the will of God. After the men were gathered up, he had a common grave dug and executed them in batches. When it was the turn of the tribe's leader, Huyay ibn Akhtab, he came forward and said, "By God, I do not repent of having opposed you, but he who forsakes God will be forsaken." Then, addressing all the men, he concluded: "God's command has been fulfilled. A massacre has been written against the Sons of Israel." Muhammad cut his head off and married his daughter, which, in context, was closer to a forced rape than a mutually consented act. How could a young woman who had just lost her entire family and community agree to marry the perpetrator of such atrocities?

This was a war crime, pure and simple, and one of the first recorded examples of ethnic cleansing. This story traumatized me and radically altered the image of a merciful Prophet that I had carried with me since childhood. Islamists still reference Khaybar as an example of Muslim might and right and have even used it as a pretense for rallying the faithful against the Jews: "Khaybar, Khaybar ya Yahud, Jaïch Mohammed sawfa ya'oud" ("O Jews, remember Khaybar because Mohammad's army is coming for you"). Khaybar is even the name given by Iran and Hezbollah to their long-range missiles!

Many more crimes can be added to a long list of atrocities committed by Mohammad and his men against women. Umm Qirfa, an elderly leader of the Banu Fazara tribe, was captured and killed "by tying a rope to each of her two legs and to two camels and driving them until they rent her in two." The poet Asma bint Marwan composed a poem decrying the murder of Abu Afak, a blind man who was one of Muhammad's political enemies. She was subsequently murdered by one of Muhammad's assassins, Umayr ibn Adi al-Khatmi, who pierced her completely through with his sword as she rested in bed, her infant at her breast. Other notably cruel assassinations include those of Abi Rafeh Ibn Abi Al Aqiq, murdered in his sleep on the Prophet's orders; Kenana ibn al-Rabi, the husband of Safiyah bint Huyay, who was decapitated because he refused to hand over the treasures of his tribe to the Muslim conquerors; Khaled bin Sufyan al-Hathali and Souwaylem the Jew, both accused of plotting against the Muslims in Madina and both assassinated in a bloodbath.

Under international law today, I could formally accuse Muhammad of war crimes and crimes against humanity, theft, rape, pillage, and destruction. The Prophet would find himself sentenced for slavery, human trafficking, pedophilia, misogyny, and bigotry against non-Muslims. In his day, of course, even his most deviant behavior was sanctioned by tradition. Knowing all that, however, it is a wonder that Muslims today can call him God's messenger, the Prophet of peace, love, and mercy.

Islam's Doublespeak

Along with criminality, Islam's other principal characteristic, formed over the last fourteen centuries, is a well-established and respected tradition of hypocrisy. The examples are legion.

First of all, Muslims welcome converts to Islam, but they forbid anyone born into Islam to convert to another religion or to simply leave the faith. Similarly, converts to Islam are not allowed to retract. Muslims consider the wars waged in the name of Islam to be lawful conquests but condemn the wars fought by other cultures against Islam as crusades and illegitimate acts of occupation and colonization. For Muslims, Spain was a savage land before Muslim invaders brought Islam, and they still regret the loss of Andalusia to the Spanish "occupiers." They are similarly outraged by France's attempt to occupy Algeria and make it "French," but they forget that it was the Arabs who were the region's first colonizers, forcing Islam on the Berbers. Their hypocrisy is equalled only by their doublespeak: whenever and wherever in the Muslim world that Christians and animists try to demand their freedom or independence, they are massacred, but the struggle of the Muslim minorities in Chechnya and Bosnia is cheered on by Muslims around the world. Another example: Islam condemns extramarital sexual relations practiced by the faithful of any other religion, calling these adultery, but the same practices are condoned and encouraged within Islam as legitimate examples of war spoils, slavery, and concubinage (*harem*). Muslims' relationships with Jews and Christians are similarly edifying. Muslims criticize Jews for calling themselves "God's chosen people" but call themselves "the best nation created for mankind." They oppress Christians for believing that Jesus was the son of God but believe that God and the angels pray for Muhammad; they deny the miracles recorded in the Torah and the New Testament, dismissing them as myths and legends, while the Quran is full of tall stories called "scientific miracles"; they decry the vengeful God of Judaism yet recite the verse in the Quran that says, "Slay the infidels wherever you catch them" (2:191). They scoff at the displays of emotion shown by visitors to the Western Wall in Jerusalem but forget that they themselves engage in their own rituals at the Kaaba at Mecca: pilgrims kiss it, circle it, and throw stones at an imaginary double before retreating to rest on a hill that was the site of all kinds of orgies.

Muslims laugh at Christians' holy water and Jews' matzo but they love their dates, camel piss, and water from the Zamzam well, at Mecca. Muslim women are forbidden to marry outside of the faith, but if a non-Muslim family refuses to let one of their daughters marry a Muslim, they are called racists.

The Quran is full of insults and barbs used against other religions, and these are repeated seventeen times a day by the Muslim faithful at prayers. Yet they are roused to anger whenever anyone insults their religion. They think that the split between Judaism and Christianity is proof that both religions are flawed. As for Islam's own internal divisions, these are dismissed as mere quarrels sent by Satan to undermine Islam's superiority. Evangelization is a threat to Islam designed to accelerate the colonization of Muslim lands, but Muslims are incensed whenever a Western country blocks the construction of a mosque.

Good-bye Islam

The dark side of Islam could fill many books. I have only provided a glimpse of what I learned by scratching its surface. My objective is not to criticize Islam, however, but to share my feelings, my experiences, my thoughts, and my disappointment, and to explain how I decided to take control of my life by cutting my ties with Islam and its God.

I assume full responsibility for this decision, even if certain questions dog me still:

Why did God create man if he didn't need him? Out of boredom? As a show of strength? Why does God get angry? How can we believe in his divinity if he behaves like a human being? How can man in his most servile and weakest form be thought to glorify his Creator?

The absurdity of this line of questioning was enough to encourage me to be done with Islam. To be perfectly honest, sharia law, which is totally out of step with the world we live in, didn't hold me back, either. Five years of research, reading, and online exchanges brought me to this point. I do not regret that I went looking for the truth about a religion that insists I accept it on a no-questions-asked basis. Today, I can appreciate the work that was accomplished through my blog and the contributions made there by my fellow seekers. The number of professed atheists in the Muslim world is rising steadily. I have to admit I take some pride from that fact.

I Am God

In March 2010, I created a Facebook page: "Ana Allah" ("I Am God"). My opening message could not have been more direct: "Ever since the death of my last messenger, Muhammad, I have watched while Mankind has sown Terror over the earth, arguing over my existence. I have decided to come to your rescue using the best means of communication known to man: Facebook. Pray for me and I will grant your wishes."

This pastiche of verses from the Quran quickly ignited the ire of some Muslims. I paid no attention and continued to post short, cadenced messages about alcohol, drugs, and other subjects familiar to adolescents. By imitating the language of the Quran, I wanted to show how, with a little wit, anyone can write a new Quran, and that Islam's holy book isn't necessarily a transcription of divine revelations.

The furor was so great that, by the end of the week, my page had been shut down. Over seven days, it had tallied hundreds of thousands of visits, and five hundred thousand people had subscribed to it. It was enough for the story to be picked up by Arab television stations, forums, and other social media networks. While these speculated as to the identity of the page's authors, I was jubilant; some thought it had to be the work of Jews and Zionists; others smelled a plot by Islam's usual enemies. There were even televised debates on the question, which amused me immensely; the author, they said, was clearly a madman who believed he was God himself.

Such a ridiculous accusation is proof of my detractors' cowardice and ignorance. They were clearly ignorant, because they accused me of simultaneously pretending to be God and denying he exists. They were also cowards because they refused to admit my argument that God is just an idea created by men.

Facebook shut my page down without checking the content for themselves, which is a breach of its own rules. A few days later, I discovered that my page had been translated into English and Hebrew, and I was proud again to think that I could make myself heard in other languages.

The whole experience led to a few more surprises. For one thing, without exception, every single criticism thrown at me by Muslims vomiting their rage had to do with sex. This just goes to show that Muslims are frustrated in general and visited my page to blow off steam. Encouraging one another to threaten and insult me—always using incredibly vulgar language and sexually-loaded barbs—they proved how easily they are led: wherever the ram goes, the unthinking sheep follow, their eyes on the ground. They encouraged readers to pour their hostility out on my page, just like they did against the Danish newspapers that published the caricatures of Muhammad, protesting, attacking, and burning Western embassies to follow the call of a few fanatical imams.

I refused to let the closing of my Facebook page discourage me. I created a few other blogs denouncing Muhammad's crimes and demanding justice. I posted less frequently, however, after a friend suggested I stop connecting from my home computer and use public Internet cafés only.

I thought I had given the slip to any possible investigators by regularly changing my IP address, which I did by connecting from different locations, and so I decided, in October 2010, to relaunch my "Ana Allah" page. In less than a month, it was an overwhelming success, just like the first one. But someone leaked my name, and I received numerous death threats by email and by phone. These always came from beyond the occupied territories or from Gaza, which reassured me, thinking they were too far away to harm me. What I didn't know was that a more serious accusation awaited me: a thought crime. I was a blasphemer!

Chapter III
Behind Bars

In early 2010, I was twenty-four years old and teaching information technology in a private school in Qalqilya. It was my first job, and I wanted
to create a certain complicity with my students, as their educator more
than their teacher. I talked about patience and tolerance with these one
hundred and fifty adolescents between twelve and sixteen years old. I was
there to help them learn and to share everything I knew, but I also wanted
these young Muslims to discover the joy of learning in an environment of
discussion, not submission. I was sure that my colleagues had passed on
their own false ideas, and I was wary of the effects this would have in my
own classroom. Fortunately, computer science and religion don't overlap.

Everything was going fine until the principal called me into his office
one day. He was upset because I had neglected to write the customary, obligatory statement, "In The Name of God, The Merciful, The
Compassionate," at the top of my exams. I kept my calm and excused
myself, explaining, rather hypocritically, that I didn't want the name of
God to end up in the trash when the students threw out their scrap paper.

As exciting as that year was, the work was considerable. One day, I
asked my class why birds are not electrocuted when they sit on an electri-
cal wire. A boy answered immediately: "It's the will of God the Almighty
who insulated their legs." I didn't know whether to laugh or to cry, so
I answered, as politely as I could: "In this class, we are studying science, where God has no place. Every observable phenomenon has an

explanation in science, and those are the only explanations I want to hear here." My students never again invoked God to hide their own ignorance.

Some time later, the biology teacher told his students that the warm seas do not mix with the cold oceans because it is God's will. My students corrected him, saying, "Mr. Waleed says we can't use God to explain what we don't know about science." I was as proud of my students as the biology teacher was furious. I congratulated them for thinking on their own and thanked them for having found the correct scientific response. I encouraged them to continue in this way, always searching for an answer from empirical observation rather than religion.

When I wasn't teaching, I was helping my father in his barbershop, where I learned the fundamentals of cutting hair. I also heard all the local gossip and learned much more.

When my contract expired at the end of the year, I found a new job in a bank, where I oversaw data input and account management. My desk job wasn't nearly as interesting as teaching, but I worked fewer hours and was better paid. I spent my free time updating my blogs. This tranquil period did not last, however.

On November 2, 2010, at nine o'clock in the evening, I was sitting at my usual computer station at the back of an Internet café, away from prying eyes. My blog was very popular in Qalqilya, and I could overhear people near me talking about it, never imagining for a second that its author was sitting next to them. I was half-listening to their conversation when two undercover officers came in and introduced themselves to me as Qalqilya Intelligence agents. They said they had come about a private affair, the details of which were unknown to them, and asked me to come with them to headquarters. They seemed to be sincere, or at least that was my impression of one of them, whom I knew personally. As I shut down my computer, I asked myself if I had done anything to provoke this summons, but I had not broken any laws or committed any crime. Could my Internet activities be the reason? All these questions went through my head without really worrying me.

In the car, the officers asked me for my cell phone. I guessed they either didn't want me to warn anyone or they wanted to look at my contacts.

Before I handed my smartphone over, I discretely reinitialized it to erase all its data: my address book, my calls, and my Internet history. The officers didn't say another word to me for the rest of the drive.

At headquarters, they told me to sit in a waiting room outside the building housing the director's office. I spent two hours—an eternity—running through the possible reasons why I had been called in for questioning and imagining what angle the interrogation would take.

What could they charge me with? My name wasn't linked to any blasphemous blogs and certainly not to "Ana Allah." As for my personal Facebook page, almost all of its visitors were from foreign countries; Palestinians very rarely connected to it, and it was mostly unknown in the West Bank, where, unlike in some other Arab countries, politics and security were bigger issues than religion in the eyes of most young people.

Eventually, an officer came and escorted me into the office of the director of the Intelligence Agency, while his security detail looked on. Some of these guards knew me personally and looked surprised to see me there: I was clearly neither a criminal nor a delinquent. The director asked the officer who had been assigned to me to close the door and to keep anyone from entering, for whatever reason. Four other officers were with him: his bodyguard, his assistant director, the director of Investigations in charge of interrogations, and the agency's director of Security.

"Do you know why you're here?" the director of Intelligence asked me point-blank.

I didn't attempt to hide my confusion and answered him that I didn't. He shot back:

"Do you think we investigate everyone who uses the Internet?"

"Of course not," I objected.

He pulled a thick file out of his drawer.

"I have everything you've written here," he said.

This time I did pretend I didn't understand.

"What writing? What do you mean?"

"Don't act like you don't know. It's my business and my responsibility to know. Do you have a Facebook account?"

"Yes."

"Do you know the Facebook page 'Ana Allah'?"

"Everyone has heard of it. It was banned, then shut down. I received invitations to join it, but I only looked at it once or twice."

"So you are neither its creator nor its administrator?"

"Me? Absolutely not."

"Let me be clear: we know with absolute certainty that you are both the creator and the administrator of this site."

"I really don't know what you're talking about."

I continued to protest, hoping to tease any information from him about what he knew and whether they had concrete evidence that would implicate me. I was starting to panic, however: I could feel my world slipping away, and I was trying not to show it.

The director asked me to come behind his desk to look at his computer screen. This didn't worry me because the "Ana Allah" page had been taken down less than an hour before my arrest; Facebook had sent me a warning, and I had forwarded it to my contacts as another example of the stupidity of social media and of the Muslims who take offense at our brand of humor. I joined him at his computer, where he was trying in vain to find it.

"The page is gone, but it was here a moment ago," he said, sounding intrigued by the coincidence. "But don't worry," he added. "We have copies in your file. Didn't you write the phrase inspired by the Surah on Abundance? 'If you are given whiskey, drink it in the name of God and offer it neat, with no mixer.'"

This parodied verse had been judged particularly outrageous by Muslims.

"And wasn't it also you who said: 'Scandal, O Scandal. What shall be called a Scandal? That you should marry a dazed, nine-year-old girl named Aisha.'"

This verse criticizing Muhammad's sexual licentiousness and marriage with the young Aisha (which I compared to an act of pedophilia) had been relayed around the world in every language via the Internet. Islamic websites had denounced it, saying Aisha had entered puberty and that Muhammad was therefore in his rights to marry her. They insisted that girls in warm climates begin menstruating early and are sexually mature at a very young age. Their arguments were completely nonsensical and ignored the Quran's own teaching, which authorizes marriage with pre-pubescent girls, in the Surah on divorce: "If you no longer expect menstruation among your women, but you are not sure, their waiting time is three months [after the pronouncement of the divorce, before the couple separates]. So also for girls who have not menstruated."

The verse clearly addresses the question of menopausal women, but since it also mentions prepubescent girls, it demonstrates that the Quran implicitly authorizes marriage with children. The verse I had written about the scandalous marriage to the young Aisha, a particularly well-turned parody, had gone viral. As a result, it had been fiercely objected to by Muslims.

"I'm sorry, I don't know what verse you're talking about. If you show it to me, I can tell you what I think."

He grabbed my smartphone and brandished it at me.

"Is this your phone? Why doesn't it have a single contact or anything saved on it?"

"I bought it two days ago and haven't had time to configure it and transfer my data."

"We're going to keep it on."

I had tried to appear dumbfounded but untroubled, even light-hearted and childish, and it seemed my tactic was working so far, gaining me a few precious hours. Tired, the director ordered me to get some rest but warned me that a very long day awaited me.

By this time, it was three o'clock in the morning. Two guards carrying kalashnikovs led me out, continuing across the courtyard and esplanade that linked the many buildings of the Intelligence headquarters. We arrived at the one that served as a prison. This was essentially an underground corridor lined with pitch-black cells, since the only light there was came from the hallway. The cells were tiny: 5 feet long by 3 feet wide. I could see that, even if there had been beds, it would be impossible to lie down.

A guard opened the door to one of the cells, gave me a small blanket, and pushed me in.

"This is where you'll spend the night. Get some rest. Tomorrow is going to be long."

He locked the door from the outside, and I was left in total darkness. I sank to the ground. I tried to gather my strength to jump to my feet, but for what? I was behind bars. After years of defending the right to free speech, I was a prisoner in a Palestinian jail. Was that the price to pay for exercising my right? For me, freedom has no price; it is life itself.

That was the first night I spent in jail. I closed my eyes to shut out the darkness. I tried to escape into my thoughts, but all I could think of was that I was locked up. What would happen to me? What were they planning for me? What would happen over the coming days? What would my friends on Facebook think? What would become of my parents, my friends and family, when the news of my arrest came out? What would people in my village think of the young man they admired and whose activities they never suspected? I remembered the reaction to the caricatures of Muhammad published in the Danish press. The cartoonist received the protection of the Danish government, whereas my government had thrown me in jail.

Why had I been targeted? They only had to go out into any street in the West Bank to hear people decrying religion, insulting their fellow man, and criticizing everything around them. I was sure that the Palestinian Authority was using me to bolster its reputation with the general public, after having been soundly defeated by the Islamists of Hamas in the most recent elections. The government needed a scapegoat to help people forget the Islamists' fatwas, which accused government leaders of permissiveness and called them traitors for trying to keep religion out of government affairs and civic life. Clearly, my arrest was designed to serve as an example of how the Palestinian Authority was doing more to protect Islam than Hamas, even if it meant trampling human rights and outlawing freedom of speech. Was I the collateral damage of a political power game or something much more serious and complex?

I was still awake when a jailer came to tell me that my questioning was to resume. Ten minutes later, two armed guards had escorted me to a car and forced me into the backseat. They positioned themselves on either side of me, and a third man sat in the front passenger seat. This was the prosecutor for the Intelligence agency: an uncultivated man, as the events that follow will show.

We were barely underway when the prosecutor turned around in his seat and began yelling at me: "What did you think you were doing? Aren't you ashamed to invent your own Quran and insult the Prophet? How much did they pay you?" I kept calm and answered him simply: "I haven't done anything wrong. Those are all lies."

He continued to threaten me until we arrived at the medical services of the Palestinian Armed Forces, where prisoners' general health is evaluated and recorded. This was a routine procedure designed only to protect investigators; it has no effect on their methods of questioning, nor does it prevent them for using torture on detainees.

I waited my turn, flanked by two guards. Two men were ahead of me, brought in by other security forces. There are seven of these in the West Bank, and all are authorized to arrest anyone for any reason. When I finally saw the doctor, he asked me a few questions: Had I been operated on recently? Was I taking medicine? Did I have any fractures or sprains? Any hearing, vision, respiratory, or cardiac problems? Without writing down a single answer or even taking the time to examine me, he finished his report: I was in perfect health. We got back into the car, but our motorcade did not take a return route; we were headed for a new destination.

When we stopped, my two guards handed me off to four soldiers who took me to a building in the middle of nowhere. I was at Military Police headquarters. The prosecutor's office was on the second floor.

The Military Police prosecutor began insulting me as soon as I entered and even tried to physically hurt me, forcing me to defend myself. The atmosphere was tense; there were ten men in the office—the prosecutor, his bodyguard, an Intelligence officer, and seven heavily armed soldiers— and all of them were looking daggers at me. The prosecutor told me to sit in a chair that was placed in the middle of the circle they formed. I felt like I was in a police movie; the scene was surreal and nightmarish.

All this time, my smartphone had been on, and the prosecutor found three new calls from foreign numbers. Worried by my silence, my contacts had left messages asking why I didn't pick up. They ended these with the usual insults to religion and god. The prosecutor asked me where these calls came from and why my phone had no contacts or saved data. I insisted I didn't know who these callers were, and I repeated what I had said in my deposition: that my phone was new and I hadn't had time to set it up. The prosecutor would have nothing of it.

"We know perfectly well that these calls are from the agents you work for, who support you and finance your crimes."

"I'm not paid by anyone."

"We have all your conversations and correspondence."

I couldn't keep from smiling when he said that, because if they really had accessed my email, they would never have tried this line of questioning.

"Why are you smiling? Do you know where you are? Do you know what's coming for you?" he yelled.

I was suddenly overcome by a wave of anger and yelled back:

"I haven't broken any law! The Constitution guarantees my freedom of opinion and expression and my right to believe what I want! You can't take those rights from me!"

"In the name of Allah, I swear you'll rot in prison for eternity and that I'll do everything in my power to uncover, dismantle, and eradicate your network forever."

In a burst of provocative laughter, I answered him back:

"What network are you talking about? Do you think the universe and the world revolve around me? How do someone's religious beliefs concern you? How can they possibly be a threat to you or to the country? Palestinian history is full of atheists who helped shape the country. I'll forgive you your ignorance because you don't know anything! Edward Said, Mahmoud Darwish, Majed Abu Sharar, Ghassan Kanafani, and Naji al-Ali were all atheists. Without their defense of the Palestinian cause, we wouldn't have a Palestinian Authority and you would be out of work!"

I regretted my outburst immediately. I had inadvertently espoused the views the prosecutor was attacking, and it would be used against me. I sat back down, feeling sorry, regretful, and defeated. Without a word, the prosecutor sat in front of his computer while the nine other agents looked on in absolute silence.

I would learn later that this prosecutor had led a six-month-long investigation to find me. The president's office of the Palestinian Authority had received a report prepared by Al-Azhar University, which houses Egypt's highest Islamic authority, and the International Union of Muslim Scholars, presided over by the Islamist scholar and television personality, Yusuf al-Qaradawi. The report asked the government in Ramallah to find and arrest the author of "Ana Allah." They were able to locate me from the IP addresses that I used.

The prosecutor's next step was to place me under tight surveillance to gather all the information needed for my arrest. He had screenshots of the "Ana Allah" page and of my conversations on Skype, Messenger, and Facebook. He knew which sites I visited, which videos I downloaded on YouTube . . . As soon as I was in police custody, he leaked my address and other personal details to the general public, deliberately putting my family in danger in the hope of coercing a confession. I think he wanted attention for this bold maneuver, to advance his career.

He never managed to break into my Facebook account, however, which I had doubly locked. The only way to open it was with both my password and an authorization by phone. Exacerbated by this impasse, he insisted:

"What do you want me to charge you with? You have attempted to destabilize the Palestinian Authority and threatened national security. You are stirring people up. That's enough to have you indicted and brought before a judge for crimes against the state."

I didn't answer him; I didn't want to risk being carried away by my anger again. Meeting only my silence, he continued his monologue, interrupted at times by calls coming into my cell phone. My contacts, my friends on Facebook, and my blog readers were becoming more and more worried by my unusually long silence on social media. Calls were coming in regularly now, primarily from Turkey, the United States, Britain, and France, and, more rarely, from Tunisia, Morocco, and Jordan. This was enough to convince the prosecutor that I was part of an international network aimed at destroying Islam. My case had become more complicated.

The prosecutor ordered me locked in an empty room in the same building, with four armed guards. They sat me in a chair and stood around me in a circle, staring me down and discussing the possible outcomes of my case. The first one to speak thought I would get a sentence without appeal. The second was more pessimistic: I might just disappear and no one would hear from me again. The third reasoned I would probably be executed to satisfy the general public and Islamic law, which reserves capital punishment for traitors. The fourth was interested in my reasons for committing such an unpardonable crime; it had to be either for money or for a woman. "They tricked you and you fell for it," he taunted me. I wondered to myself if this was all a strategy designed to get me to confess or an attempt to intimidate me for the interrogation that was to follow. On the other hand, it was just as possible that they were saying what they really thought. In any case, I didn't see anything good coming from where I was; my situation now seemed inextricable, and their comments petrified me. I was on the verge of tears. I knew I'd feel better if I cried, but not for anything was I going to let my guard down in front of them.

Inside, however, I was feeling sorry for myself and powerless. Every time my resolve would break down, I would catch myself and screw up my courage. Who were these barbarians who thought they could humiliate me like this? What right did they have to judge me? Still, I knew deep down that I was reaping what I had sown.

I remained preoccupied by these thoughts during the return ride to Intelligence headquarters. From his position in the front seat, the Intelligence prosecutor studied my file, every once in a while looking up to stare pointedly at me. I was dreading what was coming next.

At headquarters, I was locked back up in the dark, damp cell where I had spent the previous night. I was relieved to be by myself, to break the tension. I was hoping to rest and recover my strength after the long and trying day, but the guard wouldn't let me: "Tonight, you are going to spend the night standing in the hall," he told me. "Orders of the prosecutor."

This kind of punitive measure, which is not unlike a form of torture, is frequent in my country. It's used to physically exhaust detainees so that they will tell everything they know and, most important, what the jailer is hoping to hear: a confession. How many prisoners have confessed to and been tried for crimes they never committed, just to escape further suffering?

After two hours of standing completely still, and just as the pain in my feet and back was becoming intolerable, the guard's phone rang. Whoever was on the line ordered me to be brought to his office on the first floor of the building.

This office was simply decorated, dominated by a portrait of the president of the Palestinian Authority that hung over some old office furnishings and a television. The guard showed me in and left. An officer was seated behind the desk with my file spread out before him, which reassured me a little. He introduced himself as the investigator who would lead my interrogation for the prosecution. He told me where to sit down and began questioning me.

"Are you the site administrator of 'Ana Allah' and did you write articles denouncing the Prophet and Islam?"

"No," I answered.

"Then what do you have to say about this?" he shot back, showing me the evidence in my file, piece by piece.

This was a mistake, because it allowed me to see what kind of a case they had against me. There it all was, every piece of their incriminating evidence: screenshots of my Facebook and YouTube accounts and of "Ana Allah," as well as everything ever written about me online.

I admitted having looked casually at these sites, but I insisted I was neither their author nor their administrator. The investigator seemed to believe me, but he demanded I give him my Facebook password. After all, if I had seen those sites, it was proof I had an account, and if I wasn't the administrator or author, it was a normal account and I had nothing to fear. Listening to him, I began to feel dizzy. If he gained access to my account, he would see the seventy pages, sites, and blogs I maintained, denouncing Islam. He would also realize that I had known that "Ana Allah" was going to be shut down and that I had warned my contacts about it. He would read all the stories and insults I exchanged with my friends. If I gave him my password, I would be proven guilty. Worse, he would be able to see my private emails, usually to girls, some of whom lived in the city and who used their real identity in our correspondence. My contacts had trusted me: I was not going to turn them in.

I had already decided to refuse to turn over my password when the investigator interrupted my thoughts.

"Did you forget?" he asked me loudly.

I vaguely nodded while reminding him that his request was a violation of my right to privacy. My account and all its content belonged to me, and I was under no obligation to give it to him.

He reminded me that failing to cooperate with the investigation was a misdemeanor carrying its own stiff penalties. He also added, with a menacing air:

"Don't worry. I know how to make you talk."

He called the guard to lead me away.

The questioning had lasted a little more than an hour. I was taken back to the jail and made to resume my standing position facing the wall. Only a few minutes later, the director of Intelligence summoned me. The day had already been long and utterly exhausting, both physically and mentally.

Yet a new battery of questions awaited me. The director was sweeping a larger net this time.

"Does the blog 'The Voice of Reason' belong to you?"

I wondered how they knew about that page and was beginning to feel backed into a corner. I didn't deny anything, but I explained that my contributions were mostly research and hypotheses that I had developed to answer personal questions about the nature of God and Islam. He asked if I had any other blogs, but I repeated my initial statement for fear of contradicting myself.

I was thinking my nerves couldn't take any more when he handed me a print out of a blog entry announcing my arrest: "The authorities have taken into custody Waleed al-Husseini, the creator and administrator of

'Ana Allah,' the blog 'The Voice of Reason,' and others. Waleed al-Husseini is one of the most active militants and activists for atheism of the last four years." A detailed report of my Internet activities followed.

I found the strength to retort to the director that the article was taken from the Internet, where anyone can write whatever they want, often leading to unfounded, unverifiable, and exaggerated information.

He called the guard.

"Tomorrow you will be questioned by the director of Investigations himself. You will explain in detail all your Internet activities and provide him with a list of your friends, contacts, and backers. I want specific information. Do you understand? It will be dawn soon. You can rest on a couch in the meantime. But if you have something to say to me, you can call for me. I'm not going anywhere."

"I'll tell you what I know. Nothing else."

The guard led me to another room on the same floor, and I collapsed onto the couch, but he paced up and down the room so much that I couldn't relax. I closed my eyes and tried to evaluate my situation: I was in jail, and the news of my arrest was now being talked about in town and on Internet forums. I was sure my friends would rally to my defense, with the help of human rights organizations and embassies. Would their support help or worsen my situation? How were my parents reacting? And my friends? The most radical among them looked forward to a new caliphate and worldwide sharia law. Would they feel humiliated? What were my brothers and sisters telling people? How would they handle this? But my main concern was what was going to happen to me.

I don't know how the rest of that damned night passed, and I don't remember if I slept. But I remember clearly the first thing the investigator said to me when he came to wake me: "Get up and eat something. Another long and trying day is in store for you, as bad as yesterday." I hadn't eaten anything since my arrest so I tried to swallow some toast dipped in yogurt and asked for a cigarette. The director of Investigations sent for me to begin his interrogation, the real one this time. In countries where the rights of citizens are respected, individuals can be held for 48

hours until being charged with a crime. I was going to be held for four
months.

The director of Investigations began by asking me for a form of identi-
fication.

"I left it at home," I said.

"Are you Waleed al-Husseini?" he asked me.

I confirmed this, and he began filling out paperwork in silence, studying me all the while.

"Do you live here?"

"Yes, but I often travel between Jerusalem and Qalqilya."

"Why do you wear your hair long?" he asked, looking exasperated.

"Do you arrest every young man with long hair? Is that a problem? I
cut my hair when I feel like it. It's my business only."

My answer irritated him apparently, because he became very angry.

"Are you a homosexual?"

"If I were, is that a crime? But don't worry, I'm not. I like women."

"Listen to me. I don't have any time to waste with you. Just answer
my questions."

"But all your questions so far are personal."

"Are you behind the blogs and other blasphemous Facebook pages
denouncing Islam?"

"I'll repeat that I have nothing to do with these."

"And 'The Voice of Reason'?"

"Yes, that blog is mine. I publish what I'm thinking about; I don't hide
anything. I'm searching for the truth, that's all."

"Have you been paid for anything you've written?"

"No. I've never received any compensation. You can check my bank
account."

"Tell me about your Internet friends."

"They're mostly from other Arab countries."

"Are any of them Palestinian?"

"I don't know. It's possible, but everyone writes under a pseudonym
to protect themselves."

"I want the passwords to your blogs, your Facebook page, and your email account."

"That's private."

He grabbed a bottle on his desk and hit me with it. I didn't react. My primary concern was to hold up under pressure and to never give my passwords. My email account contained all my information, my pin codes, and my passwords for all my blogs, in Arabic, French, and English, as well as my YouTube account."

"Do you believe what you write?"

"Yes, I am convinced of it and I continue my thinking and my research."

"So, you aren't Muslim."

"Precisely, I am not Muslim."

"Why did you choose to write a blog rather than talk to an imam?"

"I went to imams and ulemas and asked them plenty of questions. I can even give you the names of the people I talked to. You can bring them in and question them, too."

He took the names down and then asked for the names of my collaborators, contributors, and financiers, as well as my passwords. He added:

"You are going to stay in the room next to my office. Whenever you think of a name, knock on the door. Since you are not a Muslim, I could have you killed. Islam doesn't allow me to judge an unbeliever, so I am taking myself off your case. A new investigator will be assigned," he announced.

He locked me up in what must have been his secretary's office. The window opened onto an interior courtyard where the guards on duty spent the night talking. Their discussions would prove extremely useful to me. Fifteen minutes later, a guard brought me a mattress and a blanket and told me:

"You are going to sleep here. You are in danger. A lot of people want to see you dead. You are a prisoner of the Palestinian Authority, and we don't want you murdered."

This guard was a very good man, a humble Muslim who prayed and worshipped God because of his upbringing, to face life's everyday problems. I had some interesting discussions with him. The other guard was also a good person, but he knew nothing about Islam. He never prayed, didn't fast, and cursed religion and its followers. They both treated me with respect, and their presence was a comfort to me, even though they remained my jailers and were bound by duty to obey orders.

A man I had not yet met arrived before long.

"I am the new investigator. You have an hour to prepare yourself for my questioning," he said, then went back into his office next door, leaving the door between the two rooms open.

After an hour had passed, he asked me the same questions as his colleague had that morning, and I gave him the same answers. When I refused to give him my passwords, he said he could use force to make me tell him, and I repeated that I had nothing else to say.

The coercive interrogation, a mix of both physical and psychological torture, then began. I was taken back to the dark and damp hallway in the jail and made to face the wall, but this time standing on one leg. I was allowed, however, to switch legs. From time to time, the investigator asked me if I had changed my mind. I didn't bother to answer him.

I spent most of the night like that before finally being led back to the room on the first floor with the mattress and blanket. It was a little after midnight. My back and legs hurt too much for me to sleep. Moreover, I could hear the guards in the courtyard discussing my case. It was my first glimpse of news from outside.

I listened to everything they said. According to them, I thought I was God, I talked like him, I was a traitor working for a vast international conspiracy to destroy Islam, and I was being paid to carry out my activities. I learned that the media and Internet sites were calling for my release, international NGOs were asking governments to put pressure on the Palestinian Authority to drop my case, my family had disowned me, and no one knew what the outcome would be, not even the Palestinian Authority. One of them drew this conclusion: "If the government is embarrassed and won't execute him, he'll spend the rest of his days in prison."

As discouraging as this news was, it helped me to at least gauge what was being said about me outside. Just knowing that some groups and international organizations were fighting for my release gave me a boost of confidence. On the other hand, I was stunned to learn that people thought I had been paid by an international anti-Islam network to write what I did. In the absence of any official statement by the government, rumors were flying, and this made me nervous. Were the criticisms and reflexions I had published on my blog enough to send me to prison for life? What an injustice that would be!

I also wondered if my family really had repudiated me or if that was another rumor designed to rattle me, making me think I was alone in my fight. More simply, the rumor could have been spread to protect my parents and family from being suspected of collusion or of even having known of my activities. Any refusal to accuse me on their part would have been interpreted as proof of their complicity and guilt, which would surely result in a backlash against them, from their neighbors and the city in general, not to mention the authorities. I reasoned that the best way for them to avoid being shamed in the eyes of everyone was to disown me.

Before going to sleep, I asked the investigator if I could shower; I hadn't washed or changed clothes since my arrest, and I couldn't stand myself anymore. He promised to call my family the next day to bring clean clothes, after which I could wash up.

"It's late now, and you have a long and tiring day ahead. You should go to bed," he told me before closing the door and locking it twice. Exhausted, I let myself fall asleep.

Early the next morning, I was transferred back to the basement hall-way, and the torture resumed. This time, I spent the entire day standing on one leg with my arms over my head. As he had done the day before, the investigator came from time to time to ask me the same question: was I ready to tell him what he wanted to know? At midnight, he ordered me brought to his office, where he told me that my parents had dropped off fresh clothes and that I could take a shower, but as long as I refused to talk, I would spend every day in the hallway. For the first time in several days, I took a hot shower, changed, and slept soundly.

I held out one month, standing every day on one leg. This torture was interrupted once a day when I was served my only meal: a bowl of yogurt and some bread. Every once in a while, my jailers gave me some chicken

and rice. I slept only four hours a night, when my back pain didn't keep
me awake.

The position was extremely painful to hold, and I developed a chronic
tendinitis and trembling in my arms and hands. Despite my agony, I
always listened to the guards talking in the courtyard.

I learned that Denmark was demanding my release and offering
political asylum. This was extremely encouraging news from the country that had published the caricatures of Muhammad. According to one
rumor I overheard from a guard, Copenhagen's support was proof that I
was an agent of the West at war against Islam.

They also said that imams were using me as an example in their
preaching, warning parents to keep a close eye on their children. They
were telling parents to forbid their children from using the Internet and
to make every effort to protect them from temptation, the devil, and the
enemies of the state.

"The West seeks to destroy our children and lead them off the path
of faith, to better control them. Islam is the only true religion, and this is
how the envious seek to destroy it." Such was the message being deliv-
ered in the mosques.

Imams think they are the center of the universe and that the whole
world is plotting against them and their religion. Yet why would anyone
envy Muslims their religion? For the scientific discoveries made by certain Muslims? Their contributions to culture? Or because they comprise
most of the population of the developing world? No, it's not envy that
Muslims inspire, but pity. They won't tolerate anyone calling them ignorant, yet they are the first people to deny what Muslims themselves have
contributed to science. One imam even blamed me for the lack of rain
that year: an excellent example of how ignorant Islam's religious leaders
are. If they were to be believed, my atheism brought the wrath of God
onto the entire community and led to a drought!

I also heard some guards say that my own mother had turned me in
to the authorities and had asked them to keep me locked up as long as
possible, and that the population of Qalqilya was demanding a public
execution, to make an example of me. I was more interested to learn

that human rights organizations were holding the Palestinian Authority responsible for my security, and that my friends on Facebook were leading support campaigns. Writers had taken up my case, defending free expression and the right to think and worship freely. Others reacted with surprise, however, to the idea of a growing tide of atheism in the Muslim world and demanded the Palestinian Authority stop this menace before it grew any worse. They also hoped to see the government make an example of me. A few businessmen had even put a price on my head; a wealthy Saudi proposed two million riyals and a Jordanian one hundred million dinars. By reporting constantly on these developments, Arab media and local news were indirectly sanctioning my assassination. It was a call to murder.

I was caught in the middle of these opposing factions. On the one hand, the Arab and Muslim countries were demanding my execution or at least a long prison term.

On the other, Western countries were working for my release. The Palestinian Authority needed both of these actors, politically, economically, and financially. The government couldn't satisfy both but would want to avoid angering either, putting it in an awkward position.

A month after my arrest, the director of Intelligence sent for me. I listed my grievances:

"I'm in jail, I don't know what crime I have committed, I am deprived of decent food, sleep, and basic hygiene . . ."

"Answer our questions and everything will go better for you. Your misery will be over."

"I have nothing more to say. I already told you everything I know. I want to know under what law I am being held. I haven't committed any crime or broken any law. Palestine is officially secular; my right to freedom of speech and freedom of religion are theoretically protected.

"That may be, but the first article of the Constitution stipulates that Islam is the official religion of the state and the source of its laws."

This shocked me. How can a state pretend to be secular when its constitution transgresses those very principles? I found out after my release that the constitutions of all the Arab countries were written on the same model. I wonder how true defenders of the separation of church and state in these countries tolerate this concession to fundamentalism inscribed in constitutional law. What kind of future can they really hope for when they bow to Islamists and agree to share the political arena with them? Even leftists who would call themselves progressives consent to live in backward states founded on archaic articles.

The years between 1960 and 1980 had been a period of progress and openness in the Arab world, but since then religious fundamentalism has surged in these countries, plunging them into obscurantism. The leftists and the secularists are responsible for this turn of events; they pretended to uphold freedoms but proved to be opportunists only interested in advancing their political careers at the expense of their humanist responsibilities.

This realization strengthened my determination to stop the problem at its root, by fighting religion, and Islam in particular, in the hope of sparking a popular renaissance. The slogans of the leftists and the secularists achieve only the most incremental gains. Instead, we should be shouting out: Here we are, just as we are!

I asked the director of Intelligence:

"Why do you say we live in a secular country when the Constitution itself stipulates that the laws derive from religion?"

"Your way of thinking is only good for the civilized world: Europe and the United States. It's just a slogan," he said, word for word.

"I see. But I am an atheist. Is there no article in the Constitution that respects my rights and freedom to worship as I choose?"

"Religious freedom is guaranteed to Sunni Muslims, Christians, and Jews only."

"You mean monotheistic religions. What about other branches of Islam? Don't they deserve the same right?"

I had in mind a small Shia minority in Qalqilya that had been asking for permission to build a house of prayer, a *hussainiya*, and another Muslim minority, called the Ahmadiyya, that was persecuted by the authorities. I was also remembering appalling stories where married couples accused of abandoning Islam had been forcibly divorced by the authorities. Minorities in Palestine are under constant attack, since the government violates the Constitution to serve its own ends. Freedom of worship, though a theoretical guaranty, is a relative principle. Christians are submitted to particular laws governing certain areas of daily life, such as adoption. For example, a Christian couple may not legally adopt a Muslim-born child, as he is then more likely to be raised Christian, which would be a violation of sharia law. And even though Christian groups manage orphanages and homes for the elderly and people living alone, their minority status prevents them from fighting laws such as these.

The Palestinian Constitution, like those of other Arab countries, does not uphold secularism, which implies a society that is open, tolerant, cultivated, and civilized and that is defined by social progress and modernization. These are the qualities that have placed European countries among the greatest nations on earth. In the countries of the Arab world, however, even those thought to respect secularism, Islam is not only the official religion, but the source of civil law. There are Arab pseudo-intellectuals who press their governments to apply sharia law to the letter and who work to reinstate the Caliphate. Secularism once meant something in the Arab collective consciousness, but the day is long past when the Ottoman Caliphate became a secular state under the modernizing hand of Mustafa Kemal Atatürk, in Turkey, in 1922. Today, Turkey no longer adheres to even the most basic principle of secularism, which rests on the separation of church and state and the outlawing of religious proselytism practiced by both individuals and groups.

Secularism decrees that religious instruction is optional in schools, that religion may not influence the legal statutes surrounding marriage and death, culture or communication, that religion is a personal matter that every individual is free to practice without state sanction. Ever since independence, however, no Arab state including Palestine has observed this definition of secularism.

The same can be said of Syria, Turkey, Egypt, and Tunisia, whose constitutions are based essentially on sharia law. Their presidents, ministers, and civil servants are steeped in Islamic values, through which they interpret the articles of their constitutions. Their behavior is no different in this way from that of religious leaders: they persecute and oppress minorities,

trample basic liberties, confiscate resources, and practice a generalized tyr-
anny. In short, these countries and their societies are in a regressive spiral.

In governments such as these, the ministry of Islamic assets (Wakf)
always receives the lion's share of the budget. Islamic teaching, rather
than science, is mandatory from kindergarten to high school.

Secularism will never develop in Arab countries where the population
is largely ignorant and kept in a religious straightjacket. An idealogical
current that could build a consensus around secularism and establish a
government committed to its principles is in its infancy. There's no question that, wherever secularism has prevailed, achieving it was a long and
arduous process. In France, for example, the battle was hard-fought, taking almost a century and bitter ideological debates for the majority to
agree to it.

The shouts of the director of Intelligence roused me from my
thoughts.

"Today is your fortieth day in jail, and you still haven't told us anything! By refusing to cooperate, you're only making things more difficult
for yourself!" he yelled.

"I told you everything I had to say. I have nothing to add."

"I want your username and password to your Facebook account!"

"I can't give them to you."

"Well, in that case, the investigator is waiting for you. He has something to show you."

In my very first meeting with the investigator, after I had been arrested,
he had surprised me by paging through my file while I looked on. There
were texts sent from my cell phone and transcriptions of phone calls. I
was surprised because I thought I had deleted all the contacts from my
smartphone. I had to conclude that my cell phone provider had turned
this information over to the military police and the Intelligence agency.

The investigator began by asking me about certain messages that
had been underlined in red, beginning with numbers registered in
Palestine. These numbers belonged to my father, mother, brother, and
sister, who were always asking me to run urgent errands for them and to
hurry home. Next, he wanted to know about texts I had exchanged with

people who shared my ideas. These were about navigating the blogs, content on the web pages, and thoughts about atheism, as well as some strictly personal affairs. One of these text chains was from my female Palestinian friend who wanted advice about how to improve the security of the sites, to keep out pirates and other hackers. I was devastated when I saw that. If they had intercepted that message, they had my access codes and were able to use them. All my work of the preceding years had just gone up in smoke.

After my release, I learned that the authorities had replaced the articles I had posted in Arabic with an excuse: "I ask for forgiveness from my family, my land and my country for the wrongs I have caused them, and I vow to no longer use the Internet in this way." They had left the pages in French and English untouched: more proof of their ignorance.

I didn't know any of that in the investigator's office, however. What was most disheartening was the prospect of having lost my blogs. I asked the investigator what they had done with them. He answered me curtly that it was none of my business.

"Whose number is this anyway? Your fiancée's?"

He had understood it was a woman.

"I don't remember," I said.

They had located and identified her, however, and she had been arrested and interrogated for two days by Intelligence agents, who questioned her about our relationship. She had heard of my arrest in the papers and had prepared her answer: she had only known me through my Facebook page. I can't even imagine what would have happened to her and all the others if I had given up my Facebook password. Our conversations on Facebook were of a different nature entirely, the kind that would have locked them up forever.

The investigator also wanted to hear about my correspondents in Europe, the United States, and North Africa, but he was most curious about the Palestinians who had connected with me online. They were "complicit" in my activities, he said, and he needed to find them. He was convinced we were part of a Zionist plot to rile the population, destroy Islam, and undermine national security. These accusations were extremely serious and marked the beginning of a new phase in the investigation, as well as a new level of torture and violence.

After his questioning, I was hung from the ceiling by one arm, a method of torture that, for the authorities, has the advantage of not leaving any scars. I was also blindfolded with a filthy rag, to prevent me from identifying my torturer, who showered insults on me and advised me regularly to confess, repent, and pray to God to end my suffering. I answered that God doesn't exist and is only an illusion and that I refused to pray to an illusion. My comments enraged my jailers and gave them a reason to also whip me on the bottoms of my feet.

The authorities excel at torture. My guards made me stand for hours at a time on small tin cans. The pain was inversely proportionate to the diameter of the cans; the smaller they were, the deeper they dug into my skin and the more they hurt me. After each session, I was made to run barefoot to erase the marks left on my skin.

The sessions consisted of both physical and psychological torture, administered alternately. For example, my jailers taunted me that my online girlfriend had forgotten all about me and married someone else. I didn't have a girlfriend, so I played along with their game, saying she was free to choose. Then I told them that what I had had with her was so intense that it would take them decades to enjoy even half of the pleasure she had given me. This drove them into an indescribable fury. They also tried to make me believe that my mother had asked them to kill me, to wash the family's honor, that my father had been so sickened by the strain and shock caused by my arrest that he had been hospitalized ever since, and that my brothers never left the house anymore, for fear they would be lynched by an angry mob.

I knew that my family had to be in a terribly difficult situation, one too horrible to wish on anybody. I also knew my jailers were applying psychological pressure to make me crack. Their goal was to wear me down to get me to talk. It had no effect. Two and a half months went by in this way. I took advantage of my solitary confinement to isolate myself from my environment; I lived through my dreams, my thoughts, and my hopes. In my head, I drew an imaginary space where I was completely free, and

I held onto the hope that my fight would make it possible for future generations to enjoy a space of real freedom. Our children deserved better, in a world free of extremism and respectful of individual freedoms and differences.

I found refuge in my memories and separated myself completely from the present, where I knew only torture and suffering. This was the best way I found to escape from my jailers, without any remorse. Whatever happened, I could never regret what I had done. I had no right to give up my fight. If I could live my life over, I would do it all again. Today, I can say that during that time, I grew both intellectually and morally. My experiences in jail honed the values that I defend still, and my determination to continue the fight has become utterly unshakable because of them. If I was going to die, I would rather die a hero than a coward. This was what I repeated over and over to myself, and, in this way, I found the strength to endure my situation, while vowing to defend my ideals until my dying day. I succeed at all of this despite the pressure inflicted by my jailers and the advice of everyone.

One day, one of the two friendly guards came to see me in my cell.

"I've come to talk to you as a friend who wants the best for you," he said. "Your situation has become an embarrassment for the authorities. Your case is attracting international attention, and everyone is talking about it. Even France is demanding your release. The International Red Cross and NGOs are increasing pressure on the Palestinian Authority to let you go. The Intelligence agency is reexamining your case and may close it."

One week later, the investigator assigned to my case sent for me and asked me all the usual questions. My answers were identical to my previous responses:

"I take full responsibility for the blog 'The Voice of Reason,' but I am innocent of the rest of your accusations and I have never been paid. I created the blog and wrote for it on my own initiative, following my own convictions."

For once, the investigator was calm. He wrote down what I said and asked me to sign. I read my statement and approved it with my signature. He continued:

"I want to speak to you not as an Intelligence officer but as a fellow citizen. As a citizen, I am justified to worry about national security and to work to avoid interreligious conflict. Because of my job, my worries are naturally aggravated. I sent for you because I want to apologize for your treatment, in my name and in the name of everyone who works for the Intelligence services. We will have the opportunity to talk again over the next few days, but as friends, not as an officer and a prisoner.

I asked him:

"Why and for what are you excusing yourself? I've done nothing to deserve what I have endured. I have only written my thoughts, no more and no less. You can't take it back now."

He then told my guards to feed me three meals a day, offered me cigarettes, and gave me permission to smoke whenever I wanted.

Our conversation reassured me somewhat. That night, I took a hot, relaxing shower and slept twenty hours straight. The building was quiet, as it always was on Friday, and, in the morning, I felt completely restored. Twenty hours of sleep had erased four months of torture and fatigue. Yet my mind wasn't at ease. What was behind this new treatment? Why had my jailers suddenly become so kind toward me? Was international pressure mounting in my favor? I decided I should make the most of this reversal, without budging an inch from my position.

I was transferred back to the dark and damp cell on the basement level, but it had a new mattress and the conditions of my imprisonment were better: I was allowed three meals a day, a daily shower, and smoking privileges. Two days later, I was brought back to the investigator's office, where the Military Police prosecutor was waiting to take my deposition. He was unusually calm as he asked me the same questions as before and heard the same responses. This time, he seemed to believe me and didn't ask for the password to my Facebook page.

The prosecutor told me he had examined all my bank accounts and could find nothing unusual, and he conceded that my "friends" were only Internet contacts. However, he was quick to tell me that he would charge me with unlawful dissemination of harmful ideas on the Internet.

"Many people are spreading your ideas, and it's dangerous for us. It's unacceptable, and you will be judged for your crime."

I answered that my ideas are neither deviant nor harmful and simply express my point of view, which is an invitation to accept others, no matter their differences. But he would hear none of it.

"What you want to believe doesn't concern me. You can think anything at all, but I have to charge you."

When the meeting was over, I was taken back to my cell. At nightfall, I was brought back to the investigator's office, where a new surprise was waiting for me: my father, whom I hadn't seen since my arrest, four months earlier. He appeared tired, sad, and greatly affected. By the way he looked at me, I could see he blamed me. His look said, "What have you done to us?" Seeing him so unhappy and exhausted, I was overcome with remorse for the first time. I walked over to him and put my arms around him. He broke into tears.

I sat next to him, facing the director of Intelligence, who had begun to speak:

"Here is your son. He shows no signs of torture or mistreatment. He isn't missing an eye or an ear or an arm, contrary to rumor."

"I know," my father said. "If I believed everything people have been saying I would have gone looking for him at the cemetery."

Then he turned to me and asked me how I was.

I did my best to reassure him: whatever he had had to endure because of my activism, I was the only one who should be held responsible and suffer the consequences. I let him know I had everything I needed and that I was fine. Then I asked about my mother, my brothers, and my sister. He was also careful to reassure me that my family was doing well, but I could see clearly from his look that the contrary was true: my arrest had caused trouble for all of them. I asked him to give them my love and to ask them to forgive me for the harm that I must have caused them. For the entire half-hour that we talked, my father was hardly able to say a thing because the investigator interrupted him constantly. Before he left, the ranking officer informed him that my immediate family could visit me in his office every

Saturday. This favor was confirmation of the authorities' radical change in attitude toward me. It gave me a sliver of hope but also implied that I would not soon be released.

After my father's departure, the director of Intelligence lectured me:

"Does your father deserve to be treated this way, because of what you did? You are from a respectable family and look what you have done to their prestige! I hope you are sorry for what you did. Your father only came here because myself and others intervened to convince him not to abandon you."

He was lying, obviously. I knew from looking at my father that he had tried to come earlier but had been prevented. After my release, my parents confirmed that the authorities had forbidden all visitors, fearing they would realize from my physical condition that I was being tortured. All the requests made to see me—by my family, my friends, and even journalists who wanted to interview me, including a friend who worked for an American news service—had been rejected. I also learned that two French lawyers had wanted to take up my defense, but that the director of Intelligence had not allowed that, either, telling them I didn't need a lawyer! The authorities never discussed my case, and in the silence, rumors bred and grew. The prosecutor had forbidden Palestinian media to report on my case, although everyone was talking about it.

When he had finished his lecture, the director of Intelligence asked the one guard whom I thought of as my "nice jailer" to lock me back up in my cell. He and his partner were part of two separate groups of guards who relayed each other every three days. I was fortunate to be on good terms with at least one guard in every team.

It was risky for them to be as open and friendly with me as they were, but they liked to talk until late in the night. They brought me sweets and drinks and even shared their own meals with me. They gave me news from Qalqilya, and they seemed to enjoy my observations. They were my window on the world outside, alleviating the asphyxiating isolation of my detention. Over the next six months, our discussions intensified, and, as the Arab Spring began to unfurl, we shared our interpretations of the events that were broadcast around the world. I never tired of explaining my opinions to them, and they never seemed to tire of listening to my arguments and allowing themselves to be convinced.

That night, the memory of my father's weary face stayed with me, and I imagined what my mother, my brothers, and my sister were going through. The night was short, however; at daybreak, I was brought to the investigator's office to discover a new development: the charges for which I would be tried before a military tribunal, one that was known for handing down particularly severe sentences. I was only a civilian: my case did not fall within the competence of a military court. Even more surprising were the three counts of indictment:

1. Inciting religious hatred, in violation of Article 177 of the Palestine Military Code of Justice.
2. Insulting religious leaders, in violation of Article 225 and Article 226, Paragraph B, of the Palestine Military Code of Justice.
3. Offending religious views, in violation of Article 230/A of the Palestine Military Code of Justice.

These charges were based on the Palestine Military Code of Justice from 1969, which was modeled essentially on Algeria's Constitution. The Palestinian Authority had drawn from the founding documents of many Arab countries to draft its own constitution but, in the process, saddled itself with outdated laws.

The three counts of indictment were ridiculous and confirmed how fragile the question of religion is in Palestine; it was so weak that my simple thoughts on the subject could be judged a threat. On the contrary, I had never said anything false about Islam or Muslims in anything I had written. I only quoted their sacred texts and discussed them.

For those who accused me of insulting religious leaders, I felt only disgust and pity. Religion is insulted and abused on every street corner in the West Bank, and no one pays any attention!

The third charge, that I had offended religious views, was a serious accusation because it falls under the umbrella of national security. Had I really threatened national security? On the contrary, I called for tolerance

for other religions and acceptance of differences, and I called out intoler-
ant religions that are the source of conflict. They would have done better
to try imams who incite hate and justify massacres in the name of Islam!

For a fraction of a second, I thought the investigator was provoking me
when he asked me what I had to say regarding the charges. I answered him
without hesitating: "I find them laughable, and I reject them all."

"These are the charges brought against you and on which you will be
tried. Your case is now in the hands of the judge; it is our affair no longer.
Tonight, you will stay here, because I want to talk with you. I have read
all of your articles."

At nightfall, the investigator sent for me.

"Do you know what a furor your case has caused?"

"No, I don't receive any news from outside."

"You have many friends who have come to your defense and who are
fighting for you."

"I'm grateful to them. They share my beliefs in tolerance, friendship,
and coming to the aid of others."

"Yes, but many articles that have been attributed to you were written long before you were born. Anything having to do with atheism or
that criticizes Islam and the Quran, people think you wrote; even poems
from the time of the Umayyad and containing the word Waleed."

I burst out laughing, but he interrupted me:

"Why won't you drop this fight?"

"I think it's my responsibility to humanity. I discuss the truth, as I
believe it."

"But what have you gained from criticizing religion? Did it ever occur
to you that we have bigger problems to solve, political, social, and economic? Why focus on religion?"

"Because, fundamentally, it is religion that prevents any discussion
of change and reform. Religion, and Islam in particular, interferes eve-
rywhere in our personal lives. Islam isn't a faith anymore; it's a whole
agenda: political, social, cultural, economic, and legislative. As an agenda,
it is increasingly under attack. Moreover, it's the reason why we are
regressing on human and constitutional rights! Its followers want to make

Islam the only alternative to existing political systems. Given all of that, criticizing religion is a legitimate reaction against all those who use Islam to reject secularism, modern laws, and the principle of citizenship that would guarantee equal treatment to Muslims and non-Muslims, Sunnis and Shiites, men and women. It's a reaction against those same religious leaders who threaten us constantly, condone executions, and who reject and condemn my claims! I think I have a responsibility to criticize them when they call liberals and laymen nonbelievers and traitors to Islam! We all have a duty to fight oppression and dictators, human rights violations, corruption, and the misappropriation of public funds, and we should all do so with the same goal in mind: freedom and democracy! Those of us in the Arab world who reject any religious affiliation are victims twice over: we are oppressed by dictatorial governments and by religious leaders. No democracy can survive, much less advance, when religion divides its citizens, dulls intelligence, and bases its authority on fourteen-hundred-year-old texts. Our governments are completely illegitimate military dictatorships that stay in power by violating human rights and the legitimate rights of the people. They have to be opposed, just like all the fanatics who want to replace military dictatorships with religious ones. Try to understand what I'm saying: I just want to exercise my basic rights, to think, to speak, to believe or not, and I want my fellow Palestinians to know a different culture, one of tolerance and acceptance of others, however different they may be. My dream is that, one day, religious leaders will take into account the opinions of people who don't share their views, whether they are atheists or follow another religion."

"So you're trying to convert people to atheism, just like the Islamists are trying to convert people to Islam, or evangelists to Christianity!"

"Not at all! It's never been my intention to convert anyone! I have too much respect for individual freedom and freedom of speech. I'm only saying that if religious leaders are free to defend and spread their faith, then I also have the right to express my views freely. I have the right to choose if I believe or not."

"Of course, you are free to choose," he interrupted me. "But you are not free to attack religion."

"You can't be half-free. You either are or you aren't. Believing and not believing are equal freedoms."

"Listen, I can understand your position, and maybe one day it will be accepted. In the meantime, it's late and I'm going to bed. You should, too; your trial is in two days, and you're going to want to prepare for it."

"My trial? Where and why am I going to be tried?"

"You know the counts of indictment. You will be tried by a military tribunal. I don't know which one."

"Who will represent me? Don't I have the right to a lawyer?"

"Apparently not. Those are the orders of the director of Intelligence."

The next two days seemed an eternity. It was as if time had stopped. I was extremely anxious, terrified by the idea that my case had gone to a military court rather than a civil court. I couldn't eat or sleep, and I was worried for my security above all; how many prisoners had been assassinated while being transferred to court for their trial, because they had "tried to escape?"

The day the trial was to open, the guard who came to tell me to get ready announced that it would take place at Intelligence headquarters for my safety. On the one hand, I was relieved. On the other, I was very worried about how everything would happen. At precisely ten o'clock, two armed guards escorted me to the Security building where a room had been set up for the trial. Over fifteen officers, investigators, and military personnel were seated on chairs in the middle of the room, facing a table, behind which were three men in fatigues, the military judges, seated under a portrait of the president of the Palestinian Authority and the flag. Between the judges and the audience, all of whom were investigators, were the prosecutors for the Intelligence services and the military. Guards stood around the perimeter in silence. It was an impressive scene, like something out of a Hollywood movie.

Clearly, they wanted to intimidate me, but why? One of the judges asked me to state my name, my mother's name, my date of birth, the date of my arrest, and the name of the lawyer who was pleading my case. I reminded him that I had been denied counsel by the prosecutor and the director of Intelligence. He then declared the court in session and asked the military prosecutor to read the counts of indictment. When he had finished, the judge asked me how I pleaded.

Without hesitating a second, I began by contesting the legitimacy of the military tribunal, on the grounds that I was a civilian, and an innocent civilian at that, and I rejected all of the charges. The judge studied me for a moment and declared the trial postponed to examine my requests and complaints. The court was adjourned, and the soldiers escorted me back to my jail cell. I was traumatized by the idea of having to endure two weeks of waiting, without the slightest hope.

That evening, the investigator sent for me.

"How did the trial go today?" he asked.

"I don't know if justice is the word to use when the court is stacked against me and I don't even have the right to a lawyer! They just want to convict me on the baseless charges they invented. When I objected to my trial, they postponed it, and I still don't have a lawyer!"

"We are trying to prevent your case from being formally and officially tried."

That worried me even more. They didn't want to make my trial official because I had already been illegally imprisoned for over four months. Did they think they could discreetly try my case when the whole world was talking about it?

The investigator insisted:

"It's for your protection that we have been keeping you here."

The Palestinian Authority's strategy was simple: to avoid being accused of violating my rights, it had to avoid a proper trial. But from whom were they protecting me when they were the ones torturing me? They didn't want me to have a lawyer, for fear he would mediatize a trial that wasn't even one to begin with! If my safety was what really concerned them, they wouldn't have tortured me and they wouldn't have arrested me for crimes I didn't commit, and they certainly wouldn't have brought my case to a military tribunal!

The investigator interrupted my thoughts to tell me that my parents were coming to see me on Saturday. I hadn't seen my mother since my arrest, and I had been fearing a visit from her. Because of me, she had suffered, she had endured people's unkind remarks and judgmental looks. If my father had cried when he visited, my mother would certainly collapse when she saw me, and her sobbing would leave me speechless. How could it not? I was suddenly ashamed of what I had done and what it had done to all of us. I didn't know what to feel: I wanted to see my mother, but I couldn't bear to see her sad. The investigator must have understood my confusion because he ordered the guard to take me back to my cell. I spent the following two days asking myself countless questions. How would I face my mother? What kind of condition would she be in? How would the visit go? Would I be strong enough to hold back my own tears, considering that I hadn't cried once since my arrest, despite everything I had been through? Would I give my tormentors the pleasure of seeing a weakness in me that they could interpret as regret?

The day of their visit, which had been set for nine o'clock at night, I was still asking myself the same questions. I had a knot in my stomach and couldn't swallow my daily meal. I felt weak, but I told myself I would have to overcome my fatigue and appear as natural as possible to my mother. I spent the day wondering what we would talk about and trying to imagine the best way to hide my distress from her and keep from crying. I had to help her to be strong; I couldn't break down in front of her.

At precisely nine o'clock, a guard came for me. My breathing became more labored, and my heart began to race as I approached the investigator's office where my parents were waiting for me. My feet were becoming heavier, and my knees were beginning to weaken. Just then I saw my mother, seated in front of me, her face disfigured by an uninterrupted river of tears. When I saw her bloodshot eyes, I knew that she hadn't stopped crying since my arrest, four months before. I felt as if someone was stabbing me in the abdomen. Sobbing, she took me in her arms. I stayed stiff, cold, hoping that I could hide my weakness that way and choke back my tears, which were mounting in my throat. What I really wanted more than anything was to squeeze against her, collapse into her arms, and be absorbed by her. I wanted to tell her everything I had endured: the privations, the fear, the torture. I wanted to tell her how much I had missed her and how badly I wanted her forgiveness for everything she had suffered, not because of my activism, but because of the ignorance of society and its leaders.

Her love was invigorating and made me feel like a new man. I felt invincible, ready to take on the world, protected by a mother's love, more powerful than all the world's nuclear bombs.

She held me for a long moment, and I sat close to her to let her know, wordlessly, everything I couldn't say in front of the investigator. I would only talk about two things: I would inquire about my brothers and sister and I would reassure her that I was treated well in jail.

After her initial outburst, she composed herself enough to ask a question for which she had every right to an answer: "What did we ever do for you to put us in such a mess? We did everything to give you a good education. Why did you bring these problems on our heads?"

It was painful to listen to her, especially since my parents were not in any way to blame for what had happened to me. I could only answer with silence and the sadness in my eyes.

Here again, my defense was to keep quiet even though I wanted to explain that it wasn't her fault, but rather the fault of our backward, ignorant society that is radicalized and ruled by religion. I hadn't stolen anything or killed anybody. I hadn't committed any crime or broken any law. I was only guilty of having hoped to live and speak as a free man.

I would have liked to ask her to consider for herself this absurd and unjust situation: why aren't we free to believe or not to believe? Is Islam so insecure that my atheism could be a threat to its foundations? How could my ideas and articles be considered a menace to millions of Muslims? Despite their arsenal of propaganda, couldn't they find any arguments to defend their faith and their religion instead of attacking me?

I found it impossible to say any of this with the investigator in the room, so I remained silent, and my silence harmonized with my mother's deep love, as she held me closer and closer, seeming to read my thoughts.

After having asked about my health and been satisfied by my answers, she gave me news of my family and friends and asked if I needed anything. I had to admit I missed her cooking.

The hour I spent with my parents was a shower of happiness, a breath of fresh air that gave me hope that I would join them again one day and share their peaceful home. Despite their modest means, my parents had inculcated in me priceless values, and I am immensely grateful to them.

After they left, I felt serene, and once back in my cell, I slept soundly. The next morning, I scratched onto the wall a verse from the great Arab poet, Abu al-Ala al-Ma'arri (973-1057). Each of his words summed up perfectly my state of mind and restored my confidence: "Even though I come late into this world, I must achieve what my predecessors have tried and failed to do, for unparalleled glory to be mine." I dream of reaching this goal.

As the days passed, the guards became increasingly open with me. They brought me my favorite dishes and sometimes even food they had bought with their own money. The guard with whom I had become close started to call me by a new name: Jesus! They let me phone my family three times a week, privately. Why did they break the rules for me? Were they convinced of my innocence? I'll never know, but their generosity helped me overcome most of the difficulties of life in jail. I am forever grateful for their extreme kindness.

A few days before the court was to reconvene, the investigator sent for me to pick up our conversation about my blogs. His curiosity was inexhaustible.

"Do you really believe what you've written?" he wanted to know.

"Yes, without a shadow of a doubt."

"The stories that you published, did they really happen or did you invent them?"

"They're all true. You can find them in the Sunna (the record of the sayings of Muhammad). I didn't make up anything and I didn't criticize anyone."

This made the investigator angry:

"It's impossible the Prophet ever said that only a woman or a black dog can stop a man in his prayers. It's unimaginable that the Prophet equated women with dogs!"

"If you want to know for sure, you only have to ask any imam. He'll tell you without a doubt whether the Prophet said that."

He grabbed his phone and called the imam in his village. To his great surprise, the imam confirmed my story. He hung up abruptly and turned to face me again with a comeback:

"Those are the Prophet's words, but the imam doesn't interpret them the way you do."

I interrupted him:

"Your first reaction is enough for me. Your instinct was to deny that the Prophet had said anything of the sort, because it bothered you to think so. Now that you know the truth, you're trying to say those words mean something else. You are listening to faith instead of reason, when faith and reason are polar opposites. I'll bet you aren't entirely convinced of what you are about to say to me."

"You're wrong. Whatever you say, Islam is and will always be the answer to all of our problems."

"What Islam are you talking about? Sunni or Shi'ite? Salafi or Sufi? The Islam of armed conflict or the one that the Islamist parties follow? What does that statement mean anyway: that Islam is the solution or that the solution is Islamic?"

"It means the application of sharia law in all aspects of life."

"But can Islam make decisions in politics, economics, and education?"

"Yes."

"Tell me then what Islam proposes for each! You'll see that we soon run up against its dogmatic, ideological contradictions. Take economics: certain Islamists preach socialism because they think Islam stands for justice and sharing the wealth. Yet others interpret Islam as capitalist, believing it rejects the confiscation of personal property and encourages economic liberalism. In politics, some Islamists support a democratic republic while others are in favor of hereditary monarchies. And the same kind of contradictions arise in matters of education, sociology, and the constitution! So, where is your Islamic solution in all that? Beyond these differences, how can Islam, practically speaking, resolve our political, economic, and social crises? How can it free us from dictators, corruption, oppression, poverty, and unemployment? Your answer is simple: sharia law solves everything. Yet history is full of examples that disprove your argument. The Islamists dream of restoring the Caliphate, which applied sharia law to the letter. Was that an ideal society? Is that the example we should follow to save our society and calmly build our future? Did sharia law protect the population like it was supposed to? Historians would object wholeheartedly and point to plenty of examples where, under the Caliphate, freedoms were revoked, the population was oppressed and tortured, and Muslims were robbed of their money by their leaders acting, supposedly, in the name of Islam. The Rashidun Caliphate (comprising the first four caliphs) applied sharia law, but that did nothing to improve prosperity for the general population; in fact, three of the four caliphs were assassinated during insurrections, riots, and rebellions led by Muslims. The reign of the fourth caliph was marked by the *fitnah* that split followers of Ali and followers of Aisha, in which thousands died on either side. But don't Muslims believe that when two Muslims kill each other, both go to Hell? Muslims massacred each other. The most vivid example is the invasion of Al-Harrah by the Umayyad Caliph Yazid, resulting in the deaths of thousands of men and the rape of all the women in the village. Historians say that a thousand women were impregnated. Muslims have also attacked Mecca and the Kaaba by catapulting it with stones. The journalist and theologian Abu al-Ala Mawdudi described the whole period of the Umayyad Caliphate as 92 years of obscurantism. The Abbasid Caliphate was even crueler yet. They destroyed Damas and used the famous Umayyad mosque as a stable. They killed all the men and sat on their dead bodies to eat. They spread vice and eliminated everyone who opposed their rule. Today, four countries are founded on Islam and sharia: Sudan, Afghanistan, Iran, and Saudi Arabia. We all know how human rights and freedoms are treated there; nothing more needs to be said on that subject. If that's what Islamism has done for us, tell me, when and where has Islam been a solution?"

My long speech hadn't shaken any of the investigator's convictions. He continued his argument:

"Then and now, the problem isn't Islam but its application. Islam is not responsible for these aberrations."

"That is the argument for every ideology in need of attenuating circumstances. By that reasoning, the failures of Marxism, socialism, nationalism, and capitalism are all the fault of how their principles have been applied, not the principles themselves. What is the difference between divine law and the laws of men if both can be misused? In the end, when you put aside religion, the laws that define Western society have been incontestably successful, whereas sharia law has only ever failed, then and now. Western democratic secular societies respect human rights and human dignity. Why do Islamists continue to believe that their mistakes lie in the application of their beliefs, not the beliefs themselves? Why do they persist in imposing principles that never succeed? Why do they generalize, using the errors of some Western countries to denounce Western democracy in general?"

"Islam guarantees religious freedom and belief."

"That's such a solid guarantee, it put me in jail! No, Islam only recognizes monotheistic religions, and even those non-Muslims have to meet certain conditions to exercise their freedom of religion. Legally speaking, non-Muslims are second-class citizens. Non-Muslims cannot testify in court against Muslims. If a nonbeliever kills a Muslim, his punishment is execution, but if a Muslim kills a nonbeliever, his punishment is decided by religious leaders, not the court. Insulting a nonbeliever is not punishable under the law. Nonbelievers are also not allowed to walk freely in the streets like Muslims. The Prophet told his followers to avoid greeting Jews and Christians and to fight against non-Muslims relentlessly. They must either conquer them into submission or force them to pay for protection. This is the basis of a humiliating system of discrimination. A nonbeliever does not have the same employment rights and even fewer political rights; he cannot occupy any leadership positions in the executive office of the country, the armed forces, or the justice system. Maybe these discriminatory restrictions were justified in the past, but there is no reason for maintaining them today. Yet, the same laws that were put in place by the Caliph Omar to regulate Christians living in Damas remain in effect today in most Muslim countries. Omar made it illegal for Christians to build churches, convents, or monasteries or to rebuild structures that had been destroyed by Muslims. He also made it illegal for existing churches to refuse entrance to Muslims, to ring their bells, or to display crucifixes. Individual Christians had to hide their crucifixes and pray in a whisper. Processions on Palm Sunday and Easter were not allowed, as these could disturb Muslims observing Eid al-Adha and Eid al-Fitr. They had to bury their dead in silence and avoid Muslims in the markets. They couldn't consume or sell either pork or alcohol in the presence of Muslims. They were forbidden from proselytizing, but they could not take action to prevent a friend or family member from converting to Islam. There were still other conditions imposed on nonbelievers if they hoped for any protection under the law: a nonbeliever couldn't dress like a Muslim or carry a sword, but he was required to house a Muslim for up to three days if necessary, help him, and even give him his seat. Yet he couldn't read the Quran, conduct business with a Muslim, ride a horse, or wear a beard like a Muslim. His shoes couldn't resemble those of Muslims. If he went to the public baths, he had to wear a bell around his neck to let Muslims know he was there. And if any of these conditions was not met, he were banished from the protection of Omar's government. Is that the religious freedom you're talking about?"

Before ending our conversation, the investigator asked me one last question:

"Why, in your writing, do you criticize Islam more than the other religions?"

"I was born into a Muslim society, and I understand Islam much better than the others. I write in Arabic, and most Arabic speakers are Muslim. Islam is inseparable from my life. It tries to deprive me of my freedoms and my independence, it censures my existence, and it would even decide my future and that of my children if it could. I want to live freely, and I won't let imams control my life. However, I respect their freedom to do what they want with theirs."

"That's enough for tonight. I remind you that your trial will resume in two days, at the Qalqilya courthouse."

I was fearful again as I was led back to my cell. I had no idea why the location of the trial had changed.

The day the trial was to resume, I woke early. Two armed guards came for me with handcuffs to lead me, wrists and ankles tied, to the car that was waiting to transfer me to the Qalqilya courthouse. I felt humiliated and I fought back. I refused to be treated like a criminal and be judged by an illegitimate tribunal. The two soldiers lost patience and tried to overpower me with their fists but the guard stopped them, reminding them they were not allowed to use violence and brutality against me, on the orders of the director of Intelligence. Five minutes later, he appeared in person to explain that the conditions of my transfer were no different from those of any other prisoner; they were simply meant to prevent any attempt at escape.

I reminded him that I was not a criminal, that I had committed no crime, and that I had no intention to escape. I wanted to be brought to the courthouse on my own, without any escort. The director of Intelligence would not be swayed: "All prisoners are handcuffed during transport." I was equally intransigent: "I'd rather stay in my cell and miss my trial than be handcuffed."

The director began to tremble with rage. He couldn't take the risk that I would refuse to be transferred to the courthouse, but he could not forcibly handcuff me, either. Finally, he relented. It was a moral victory, but an important one for me. For the first time since my arrest five months earlier, I was leaving Intelligence headquarters, which had become my prison.

Through the windows of the car, I watched people in the streets and observed my own impressive escort. There were Intelligence agents in vehicles just ahead and behind mine, while two Palestinian police cars cleared the road and two more brought up the rear. The atmosphere was tense. The drivers carried handguns and the others held kalashnikovs. Our motorcade drove at full speed down deserted streets through intersections that had been cordoned off by the police. The entire neighborhood around the courthouse had been sealed off; not a single civilian was allowed access, courthouse employees had been asked to leave, and the general public was kept at a safe distance and forbidden from filming the motorcade as it passed. Every precaution had been taken to prevent me from having any contact with the outside world. I asked one of the guards the reason for these security measures.

"More and more people are demanding your execution," he told me. "There is a bounty on your head. The authorities want to protect you."

I was amazed to think that my motorcade's security rivaled the president's or the prime minister's. In the streets behind the barricades, people were trying to catch a glimpse of the occupants of this convoy that was driving at breakneck speed with armed escorts. Inside the courthouse complex, two rows of police officers formed a human corridor leading to the building. It, too, had been evacuated, and sharpshooters had been posted on the roofs of surrounding buildings and in the windows of the courthouse.

The two armed guards led me to the courtroom. The new judge who was waiting for me asked the soldiers to leave the premises, saying that justice could not abide the presence of guns. I was sure that this judge would be fair, unlike the first one, and I was not proved wrong. He told me to state my name, my age, and my address, then asked if I had anything to add. I repeated again that my case had no place in a military tribunal. The judge asked the military prosecutor to explain, but he only responded with the usual argument:

"What you have done is very serious; it affects the Palestinian people and threatens society. Your case is therefore a matter for the military courts."

The judge looked at me with surprise.

"I read your file, but I didn't fully understand it. What did you do, exactly?"

"I had a blog where I thought through my questions about Islam and published articles criticizing it, based on philosophical and existential ideas."

"You had doubts and you wrote about them on your blog?"

"Exactly."

"You do not belong in jail. Your father has to request your release and I will sign it."

Disavowed, the military prosecutor reacted immediately, hoping to prevent my release. He repeated that my case had not been decided and that, until it was, I needed to remain in jail, where I would be better protected from death threats.

The judge asked me what I thought.

"I have been jailed for five months. That is much longer than any investigation could last. As for these supposed death threats, they are designed to frighten me and keep me in jail."

The judge then asked the prosecutor to close the investigation and to submit his report by the following day so he could examine it and make a decision. Then he turned to me:

"Tell your father to make a request for your release, so I can sign it at the next hearing. You will still be required to respond to all summonses and to be present at your trial."

The joy I felt was immeasurable. The judge's decisions seemed to be free of any political considerations. I was sure he would decide independently and fairly on my case, according to questions of the law and no others. This was unusual.

When I left the courtroom, two police officers came toward me with handcuffs. Instinctively, I froze. The guards from the Intelligence agency intervened and told them I was under their protection. Conflicts between the different security services of the Palestinian Authority—Police, Intelligence, and Security Forces—are not rare, as these often have competing interests. The power struggles between them can be ferocious. Each of the three services is at pains to demonstrate its importance, going so far as to invent cases against innocent people, to justify its existence and its budget. How many people have been falsely charged with working for Israel and imprisoned for years before being proven innocent? How many innocent people have been accused of murders committed while they were in prison? Endless reserves of imagination have been exhausted by government employees to justify these arbitrary arrests.

None of these services had hesitated for a minute to use the rumor mill to incriminate me in my own city. According to some of these rumors, international NGOs had paid me handsomely for my writings. Others said I was the head of a secret organization trying to destroy Islam. Still others declared I was plotting an anti-Islamic revolution, with the help of Freemasons and Zionists. Yet another pretended the Danish cartoonist who had made headlines in the Muslim world a few years earlier had adopted me and that his daughter wanted to marry me! A society must really be sick to feel the need to spread such outlandish rumors.

The motorcade took a different direction as we left the courthouse. When we arrived at Intelligence headquarters, the director summoned me to his office.

"How did the trial go?"

"I hope to be released at the next hearing."

"Perhaps, but your safety is compromised by death threats. The court does not have the last word. Your case concerns national security."

"The judge's decision has no weight?"

"I repeat: he is not the only one who must decide on your case because what you have done is very serious."

"But I haven't committed any crime! The Palestinian Authority says, officially, that it is democratic and secular. Well, is it or isn't it?"

"That depends on what you think 'secular' and 'democratic' mean."

"Democracy is a system where everyone participates in decisions! Democracy refuses to allow a minority to decide for the majority, but it does allow the opposition party to be elected. That's called a change in power. Without those conditions, democracy has no chance. Secularism, however, guarantees that these conditions be met. It makes it possible to integrate citizens no matter what their faith is. It guarantees equal rights and protections on the basis of citizenship, not on religious affiliation or gender. It guarantees that laws and constitutions are adapted to society and not to religious principles like *halal* (lawful) and *haram* (forbidden)."

"Of course, some of what you say is true. . . I even think that if you said only that, without ever calling yourself an atheist, people would listen to you. The problem is that, since you shout from the rooftops that you are an atheist, no one wants to have anything to do with you."

"You'd like me to be a hypocrite and pretend I don't believe what I do, but my goal, precisely, is to light the spark that is essential for change to happen. Secular Arabs have been fighting for decades, in vain; they never succeeded at changing people's minds. They only attacked the surface of the problem; they never got to the root. Their failure left the road wide open for religious leaders, who indoctrinated society and kept it ignorant of the world. It's time to attack the problem at its root, and that is religion, Islam in particular. We need a cry of revolt to set things straight. That's what I wanted to do."

"Our society rejects Western ideas. It's an ancient conflict between our civilizations: Western values are incompatible with ours."

"Good ideas know no borders. There's no such thing as a Western or an Eastern way of life. Values and principles are human; Western values can survive and prosper in a Muslim society, and vice versa. Democracy, good governance, human rights, mutual respect: these are purely human values that belong to no one religion or race. They must be upheld, not contested under the false pretext of protecting the principles and values of Islam. The Arab world is increasingly under the sway of religious sentiment, particularly since the Arab Spring. Even in Palestine, more people are followers of Hamas since it developed a religious discourse."

"Let me tell you what I think: you are educated and your arguments make sense, but you will always be undermined by your atheism. You are and will remain a traitor to Islam. Go back to your cell and see what the future holds for you. If you want, I can authorize some distinguished representatives of the city, imams and university professors, to come speak with you."

I accepted his offer and returned to my cell, his final words ringing in my ears. For me, there is no question that the discourse of Islamist movements, with their foundation in religion, is radicalizing Arab societies, which are by nature sentimental and pious and therefore easily swayed by religion. Any imam can call a mob to arms with a simple, well-phrased sermon. What's more, the rise in Islamist movements in the 1970s was a reaction to similar growth of Jewish, Christian, and Hindu movements.

Despite their ideological and intellectual differences, all of these radicalized movements share a common objective: to wipe out all other faiths,
to eliminate any ideas that are contradictory to their own. It's time for our
countries' intellectuals and elites to join together to bring society into the
age of progress and change religion's tone. The Islamist agenda is incompatible with human rights and modern society. There are five reasons why.

To begin with, under Islamism, *theology is an omnipresent abstraction.*
Radical Islamist movements use religion to fight competing ideological
movements. They can find no better response than to propose Islam as
the solution to everything. For them, it is a symbol of national identity,
culture, and civilization and is consequently at the center of any project
to develop Arab civilization. How much easier it is then for the Islamists
to galvanize people with their slogans, as the tele-Coranist Yusuf al-Qaradawi did when he declared, "Islam is the solution that goes to the root
of the problems instead of treating the symptoms only." Despite his discourse, he has no practical solutions to offer. Sayyid Qutb takes the same
line, arguing: "Ideal Islamic society reaches around the world. It belongs
to no nation or race and knows no borders. It welcomes all people." This
idea was discredited by the Islamists themselves, who never stop group-
ing people into categories with different rights and duties, sowing divisions between Muslims and non-Muslims, between Sunnis and Shi'ites,
between Salafists and Sufis, between men and women, between those
who believe and those who do not. Islamists are convinced that they alone
represent the identity and the culture of the nation, and so they take it
upon themselves to eliminate any other way of thinking. They say, "The
salvation of the Nation relies on Islam, which keeps it safe and opens
the gates of Paradise" (Al-Qaradawi). Such a grandiose statement only
excites people, while promising nothing in the way of political, social, or
economic policy. Islamists are quick to reference sacred texts to sanctify
their argument, even though history proves them wrong, again and again.
Under Islam, there are no protections in place to prevent any leader from
using sharia to oppress the people, as the caliphs did.

The second problem with the so-called Islamist solution is its *religious
dimension,* which lies at the heart of Islamist propaganda. Muslims are

enjoined to devote their lives, their health, and their work to their Creator and to seek out God the Merciful and Compassionate for any problem, which is in itself a practical expression of the Islamic solution. "Any constitution that is not in conformity with sharia must be considered an affront to God" (Al-Qaradawi). Such a purely religious stance should have no place in political questions because the Islamic solution rests not on its ideas, but on its supposedly divine nature. Al-Qaradawi sets the superiority of God and his laws against civil law, which must by nature be inferior.

The incursion of religion into politics introduces other serious problems. While there is no true democracy that is not opposed by a minority, Islam, however, is based on the principles of *halal* and *haram*, which the Islamic parties use to declare themselves *halal*, as defenders of the faith, and their opponents *haram*, and therefore outlaws. No peaceful cohabitation is possible between them, since the Islamists consider that their adversaries are impious deviants.

The third problem with the Islamist solution is its *lack of a program*. Islamists have no political vision for our social crises. Consequently, they refuse categorically to debate their opponents as long as these groups purport to lead without having recourse to Islam. Paradoxically, certain Islamists use their lack of a program to their advantage, as it widens their appeal. The situation becomes unmanageable with so many different parties under the Islamist umbrella defending their own ideas and imposing their own solutions, leaving a multitude of propositions, all of which are based on Islam and all of which are theoretical and inapplicable.

Another problematic matter under Islamism is its *discrediting of everything non-Muslim*. Islamist discourse seeks to marginalize other ways of thinking and eliminate these. It goes at this by disfiguring and weakening philosophical concepts, political and social currents, and economic theories that run counter to its own principles. Marxism rhymes with atheism and is therefore condemned. Darwinism reduces mankind to an animal. Freudianism is obsessed with sex. Existentialism is the mark of an intellectually sterile mind. Capitalism is simply materialism. Every idea and theory coming from Western thought is deemed either deviant or criminal and must be banned.

There are two reasons why Islam takes this approach of discrediting counterphilosophies. On the one hand, Islamists are as arrogant as they are ignorant, which prevents them from debating and accepting opposing ideas. On the other, they know that by misrepresenting those ideas, they can better mobilize the faithful to reject them and everything they represent.

Finally, the Islamist solution is impracticable in any democracy because of its *isolationism*. The primary feature of contemporary Islamist discourse is the fear of interacting with other civilizations. Religious leaders think they can defend the authenticity and the superiority of Islam by rejecting outright any mixing with other currents of thought. However, they only manage to isolate Muslim societies from scientific, intellectual, and cultural developments and wall them up in their ignorance. Sayyid Qutb taught that all schools of philosophy and psychoanalysis, all interpretations of human history and society date back to *Jahiliyyah*, a pre-Islamic period of barbarity and ignorance before the revelation of the Quran to Muhammad. Consequently, he argued, these theories are by nature hostile to religion in general and to Islam in particular. While Qutb may have said that science is not defined by any nationality, religion, race, or gender, he rejected the application of the sciences to the human condition and their philosophical and metaphysical interpretations, which, he said, were part of the great Jewish plot to destroy Islam.

On that basis, he rejected all other civilizations and all other political structures, as well as all revolutionary movements and their principles: the Magna Carta, the French Revolution, American nation-building and its individual freedoms. For Qutb, these aspirations toward new structures of governance limited their range of application by placing their focus on universal human values, rather than on the divine.

Abu al-Ala Mawdudi argues, however, that Islam and sharia define a global way of life, beyond just theological, ideological, or religious questions, and that everything that does not fall under those global laws is illicit. Sayyid Qutb pronounced a total rupture between Islam and the rest of the world when he wrote: "The world, its principles, its ideas and its values come from *Jahiliyyah* (ignorance) and are therefore incompatible with Islam."

Islam's identity rests on the rejection of all other civilizations. The Lebanese cleric Fathi Yakan declared this in plain and simple terms: "To believe that the future belongs to Islam is the same as admitting the weakness and failure of all other concepts. Capitalism, democracy, Socialism and Communism have all failed because they are constrained by time, whereas religion is timeless."

In the interim, I wrote to my father asking him to come to the next hearing and to make a formal request for my release. I was also allowed visitors, one of whom was my aunt. She lived with my family and was like a second mother to me. She was very pious and read the Quran daily, even though her eyesight was poor and she feared losing it. This loving and respectful woman forgave me for my writings criticizing Islam. She had been a brilliant student herself, but her parents, in accordance with tradition, insisted she stay at home. She did learn a craft, however, and had become one of the best seamstresses in town. My arrest had provoked the anger of this honest and intelligent woman; in her opinion, God alone had the authority to judge me.

She was also very sensitive, and, as I expected, her visit was accompanied by many tears and an uninterrupted stream of questions about my health and my treatment. She had been frightened by rumors that I had lost an eye and part of my ear under torture, so she insisted on feeling me all over to make sure I was unharmed anywhere. I even had to lift my shirt for her to see for herself.

My mother and my aunt also brought me a coat in which they had hidden food they had prepared for me. The security guards did not let the coat in, however, and I was sure that, after having searched it, we would never see it again. Nevertheless, one of the guards finally entered, the coat in one hand and the food in the other. The investigator became enraged: "It is forbidden for visitors to bring food for prisoners, especially him!" However, my mother insisted that I try some.

"What proof do I have that this food isn't poisoned?" the investigator shouted at her. "I can't take the risk that Waleed dies in jail."

"You can't be more concerned for my son's life than I am," she replied.

"I am only following the rules. Visitors are not allowed to bring food into the jail."

"I want to see the director. I will eat some myself to prove to you this food has not been poisoned, but I prefer that Waleed eats it."

I had never seen such determination in my mother, who was normally so reserved. The trials she had suffered during my arrest had clearly changed her. The investigator picked up the phone to call the director of Intelligence but wasn't able to reach him. My mother had no intention of leaving with the meatballs she had prepared for me, so, without a thought for the investigator's reaction, she fed me a few, which I gladly devoured!

After they left, the investigator launched into a speech about following the rules and respecting others. I replied I could take any abuse for just a few of my mother's filled pastries.

The following day, the director of Intelligence sent for me. I thought his summons must be in relation to the events of the previous day, but something entirely new was in store for me.

Four men dressed in white with full beards were in his office. They were local Salafist leaders who had come to set me straight. They introduced themselves, one at at time, for five minutes each and reminded me of the benefits of religion, the wisdom of the Prophet, the fairness of Islam, and the power of God, creator of the universe. They assumed I had never read the Quran and that they had been invited to explain it to me in order to save my soul. I told them I knew two-thirds of the Quran by heart, that I had read the commentaries and the Sunnah, and that I was ready to discuss it with them. For example, I asked, jumping right into it, could they explain for me where the sun goes when it sets?

Their response: "It sets between the hands of the Creator and rests in a shelter of mud until God commands it to rise again."

"Really, your answer is stupid and naïve," I countered. "The sun doesn't move at all; it's the Earth that turns around the sun. I don't want to get the director of Intelligence involved, but I'm certain he's not so gullible as to fall for your little joke."

The director of Intelligence jolted awake enough to mutter:

"Ask our Merciful God for forgiveness. You are the worst kind of miscreant. I won't allow you to make fun of the Quran in front of us."

"I'm not making fun of the Quran; I'm telling you the truth. Prove to me that the Quran is authentic."

"The proof is in the Quran!"

"How so?"

"The Quran has survived fourteen centuries without a single change. It has been passed on from generation to generation in this way: it has never been modified, not even in the slightest way."

"How do you know? Who told you?"

"In the Quran, the Prophet says, 'Indeed, it is we who sent down the Quran and we will be its guardian (Surah Al-Hijr).'"

"That's illogical. It's the same thing as accusing a thief of stealing, then letting him go, on the basis of his own denial. There are literary works and whole epics that date back to before Islam and that have been passed down untouched over the centuries. I ask you for proof that the Quran is authentic, and you tell me the Quran says so, so it must be. Your answer is nonsensical."

The imams said they would bring me proof, then began to threaten me:

"Your murder is justified and when you are dead, you won't be buried in a Muslim cemetery. We will instruct you over the next three days. If you return to Islam, you will be saved. If not, you will be executed! You are possessed by a powerful demon."

I hoped the request for release that my father was preparing would be granted. However, when the trial resumed, I discovered to my great consternation that the judge had been removed from my case and replaced by a magistrate who had ties to the government. I knew then that the Palestinian Authority had brought the justice system to heel through its various security services, proving once again that the Palestinian state was the furthest thing possible from a democracy.

The judiciary is the spinal column of the state, on which the safety and
the security of society depend. Impartial justice is indispensable to nation
building because it is the very essence of the modern state and responsible for keeping it honest. Our leaders owe it to us to protect the judiciary
from tyrannical tendencies and to rid itself of magistrates with partisan
interests. That day is still far off, however.

The president of the Palestinian Authority can say what he wants, but
our justice system is not independent. While I was in jail, he claimed that
there was not a single political prisoner in a Palestinian jail because all
the prisoners were criminals or militants fighting to disrupt the state. He
hoped to reassure his foreign partners and win over public opinion, but
my trial was proof enough that he was lying.

In the courtroom, I had the feeling that things were not going to go
well for me and that I would no longer enjoy the clemency of the former
judge nor see my request for release granted. The magistrate asked me:

"How do you plead?"

"I reject all the charges on which I stand accused. They have no basis
in reality; they have been fabricated entirely. I have not committed any
offense, misdemeanor, or crime."

"How is that possible? Didn't you say that the Prophet slept with his
servant in his own marriage bed?"

"Yes, I said that, but I didn't make it up. It's in the Quran, in the Surah
At-Tahrim (The Prohibition). According to Abdullah ibn Umar, the
Prophet was with Maria al-Qibtiyya, his concubine, in the bed he shared
with his wife, Hafsa bint Umar. When Hafsa discovered them there, he
begged her to keep it a secret from his other wives, but in exchange she
asked him to never touch Maria again. Hafsa told Aisha anyways, who
confronted the Prophet who had already slept with Maria again."

"That's not surprising; deception is the rule in this story, as you know
full well!"

"But the Prophet, to justify what he had done, invented a Surah. After all,
the angel Gabriel is always ready to supply one, isn't that right? 'Prophet!
Why do you forbid that which God has made lawful to you, seeking to
please your wives? God is infinitely clement and merciful. God has already

absolved you of your oaths. He is your Guardian, the Omniscient, the All-Wise.' The Prophet disclosed a secret to one of his wives, who divulged it. God made it known to him who told his wife. She demanded to know: 'Who told you this secret?' He replied, 'The Omniscient, the All-Wise, informed me of it.' (Surah At-Tahrim 1-3). But why didn't God warn the Prophet that Hafsa was incapable of keeping a secret? None of it makes sense."

The judge spoke again:

"I forbid you to tell this kind of story again before the court."

"Are you trying to deprive me of my right to defend myself? I have done nothing wrong by speaking the truth. If you don't want to hear these stories, you'll have to remove them from the Quran."

"So you insist on persisting in your criminal arguments?"

"I am not a criminal. My words come directly from the Quran and the Sunnah."

"Can you say the same thing for the verses you rewrote and published on your blogs?"

"Doesn't the Quran ask the faithful to invent new verses? Then how can you forbid me from doing what the Quran authorizes? I wouldn't say my verses are better, but I'll let readers decide for themselves. If they think they are ridiculous, then my verses will reinforce their faith by proving that nothing can equal what is written in the Quran."

"I am adjourning the court so I can look over your case. The trial is postponed until next month to allow me time to question the witnesses. I am rejecting your request for release. You will remain in prison until the end of your trial."

I was taken back to my cell. I saw no hope ahead, only many more months in detention.

During the seven months I had been detained, Arab dictatorships had been challenged by revolutions that demonstrated that our societies could no longer continue as before. In the beginning, these uprisings expressed simply the rage of famished citizens or were *intifadahs* against corruption and hardship. These mutated as they grew, however, toppling regimes and exposing the weakness and opportunism of the opposition parties who thought, wrongly, that ousting a dictator was enough, when it was only the first step toward democracy.

Some members of the opposition parties who had forgotten how many people had died under these dictators were unprepared for the violence of the government crackdown. These parties had little structure and less power than the dictatorships, and, despite their failings and weaknesses, they maintained their interdependent ties with the government. To build a revolution that would last, they should have started by educating people before they began overthrowing the existing regimes. This is where the elites and the opposition movements could have made a difference. Instead, they were too divided and weak to be effective. Rather than overthrowing the dictators, they gave them new life.

I followed the Arab Spring from my cell, wondering all the while why the Palestinian people never got into step with Tunisians, Egyptians, Libyans, Yemenites, and Syrians. Palestine, however, which lacks democracy, freedoms, and the rule of law and which is hampered by its unsuccessful fight for self-determination, has always had to bear more hardship than the other countries of the Arab Spring and always will. The Palestinian Authority's failure to achieve statehood had undoubtedly inoculated Palestinians against hoping for their own revolution. Their priorities look nothing at all like those of their Arab neighbors.

In Palestine, the idea of legislative and presidential elections is practically a utopian quest because no one is interested in organizing open and fair elections. Disagreements paralyze the whole political system. Hamas grabs power in Gaza, Fatah discredits everyone else in the West Bank, and Palestine sinks deeper into an unprecedented, existential dead end, with economic and security crises, to boot. A majority of Palestinians live below the poverty line. Unemployment rates in the West Bank are over 20 percent and in Gaza are as high as 35 percent. Growth depends on international aid, and our few exports rely on the good will of Israel and the occupation of vast swaths of territory. According to the International Monetary Fund, the Palestinian Authority is not ready for independence or sovereignty, despite the government's triumphant slogans. The crisis of confidence between the people and their leaders only deepens.

While the Arab world rose up, I was powerless, in jail. Life was going on without me; I felt useless.

One day, the director of Intelligence sent for me. He had received the judge's detailed report of the hearing and wanted to question me about my acerbic exchange with him.

"You only make your case worse by insulting Islam and criticizing the Prophet. Calling him a sex maniac only inflames everything."

"I am not insulting or criticizing anyone; I am simply describing the situation."

"You have to respect Muslims' faith and beliefs."

"Only when they remove from the Quran their own insults directed at other religions, only when they get rid of all the Surahs that call Muslims to battle and to convert the rest of the world by force will I respect Islam. How can you ask me, who have rejected Islam, not to react when I am woken every morning by the call to prayer and when I hear imams drag my name through the mud and demand my execution?"

"You mention whiskey in your verses when you know alcohol is forbidden to Muslims. Don't you realize that you are making fun of the Quran?"

"I only did that in the beginning. If I had continued to write satirical verses, I would have written better ones probably. You know as well as I do that alcohol was not forbidden initially, only later, which is proof again that the Quran was invented by men. Islam adapted to its environment by modifying its sacred text. Ibn Taymiyyah used to tell his disciples: 'Use the verses revealed at Mecca when you are weak and the ones revealed at Medina when you are strong.' This is what Muslims are doing today all over the world: when they are weak and in the minority, they fall back on proselytizing, and when they are strong and in the majority, they use force. That is what's happening in Iran and Afghanistan today."

"That's your opinion, but you have to stop insulting and clashing with people who don't share your views. A professor of biology at the university is going to come to see you tomorrow. He is a specialist in the evolution of the species at the prestigious Palestinian university An-Najah. I hope your conversation will be constructive. He insisted on meeting you."

Before I left, he added:

"Oh, and I also wanted to tell you that I gave your father permission to bring you food."

I was happy to have a visitor. The next day, the professor arrived. He was the chair of the biology department. He told me he wanted to meet me to let me know what had been happening outside. In particular, he said, my photo and my case were being used by certain ill-intentioned people to undermine Islam.

I interrupted him immediately:

"There is no plot to overthrow Islam, and what I did has nothing to do with politics. I am only trying to find the truth. If the authorities hadn't arrested me and thrown me in jail, no one would be able to capitalize on my case for their own ends. Instead of torturing me, the authorities could have tried reasoning discreetly with me, and the whole thing would have remained a private matter."

"That's possible, but what's done is done, and the situation has changed, too. It's in your best interests to repent and ask for forgiveness because you are endangering Islam."

"You want to impose Islam on me by force just like the early Muslims?"

"I didn't say that. I only want the West to stop taking advantage of your case. I studied in Great Britain, where I got to know many atheists, but I began my doctoral thesis with the Quranic verse about the development of the fetus (Al-Mu'minun—The Believers, 12–14): 'Certainly did we create man from an extract of clay then placed him as a drop of sperm in a firm lodging. Then we made the drop of sperm into a clot of blood and we made the clot into an embryo from which we made bones that we covered with flesh that we made into a new creation. Blessed then is God, the best of all creators!' It explains the miracle of birth before modern science became interested in the question. Instead of turning your back on Islam, you should learn to appreciate what it can teach us, especially in the sciences."

"There is no 'Scientific Miracle' explained in the Quran," I replied. "It's a ruse to hide how outdated the Quran is and its contradictions with modern science. Moreover, if you translate your verses into a modern language, you will see what their true meaning is. For example, to say: 'We made bones from the embryo and covered them with flesh' makes no sense, because bones and flesh develop simultaneously. These verses were meant for an uneducated population and were written in simple language for the common people to understand. Take pregnancy, since you mention it. The Quran offers a simplified explanation and speaks of coupling without ever mentioning that, for a fetus to form, an egg must be fertilized by a spermatozoon. The Quran merely repeats the commonly received idea at the time that a man's liquid mixes with a woman's . . . That's false, yet Islam has holed itself up in that lie for centuries!"

We had nothing more to say to each other, so the professor left, and I returned to my cell.

When my parents came to see me again, my mother brought my three favorite dishes, which she had simmered for two days and were especially delicious. Before I allowed myself to devour them, however, I asked my father why he hadn't attended my hearing. He told me that the new judge had not allowed him to enter the courtroom, but that he had made a new request for my release anyway. Nevertheless, the judge wanted to keep me in jail and also wanted to call four witnesses to testify against me. According to my father, one of these was the owner of the cybercafé where I used to access my blogs, and the other was one of the regular clients there.

In the meantime, the days passed, following the same routine, except that I was no longer allowed to speak to anyone. Finally, I was moved to the main courthouse, which I entered, escorted, through a back door. The courtroom was packed, and I had to wait in a specially secured area, away from the audience, which was composed mostly of people curious to finally see who I was and judge me on that basis alone. I had been headline news for the last seven months, and people were discussing the possible sentences the judge could deliver. Rumors were evidently still circulating, as well, that I had been paid by Western countries for my articles.

A police officer led me before the judge, to whom I was asked again to present myself. The hearing would last over three hours. After the counts of indictment were read, the judge called the witnesses to the stand. The first was the director of Investigations, whose presence at the trial was a violation of the law that says that military personnel may not testify in a case involving a civilian. Everything in my case was illegal, however: my arrest, my preventive detention lasting over seven months, my emotional and physical torture, my judgement by a military court, and, now, a witness who was none other than the investigator in my case!

After he took his oath to tell the truth, the judge began to question him:

"Did Waleed ever admit to you that he was guilty of the charges against him?"

"Yes."

The judge then asked me if I had anything to add. I protested the witness' statement:

"The witness claims that I said I was guilty of the accusations, but I have never recognized any of the charges against me. On the contrary, I can only laugh at them. What I said during the investigation was that I had a blog: that's all. A blog where I defended the separation of church and state and the values of a civil society, while exercising my freedom of expression that the Constitution has guaranteed. I wrote about religion without ever fanning religious differences or offending anyone. Everything I wrote and published comes from your books. Why is it forbidden to speak of Muhammad as a man and not as The Prophet? Why are you so afraid of the truth when it can open your eyes to the lies and legends of religion?"

The judge asked the chief Investigator if he had obtained my confession under torture or threats. He denied using force in his interrogations. The judge then asked me to speak.

"First of all," I began, "I never admitted to any wrongdoing. Why do you insist on saying that I confessed? Secondly, I was tortured during the first four months of my detention. How can you deny it?"

The judge pretended he hadn't heard my request and instead read aloud a text written by the Intelligence services to incriminate me and prolong my incarceration. Clearly, my case had already been decided;

the judges were not independent, and justice would not be served. He thanked the first witness and moved on to the second: the manager of the cybercafé where I used to go before my arrest. He swore to tell the truth, and he did.

The judge asked him:

"Is Waleed the owner of the Facebook page 'Ana Allah'?"

"I don't know. People say he is, but, personally, I can't say for sure. I saw him reading the page sometimes, but that's all."

"Did you ever see him write any satirical verses?"

"No, never."

"Is he the owner of the blog, 'The Voice of Reason'?"

"Yes."

The judge then asked me if I had any questions for the witness. I replied that the witness had confirmed my own statements—that I had nothing to do with "Ana Allah"—and that I had nothing more to add.

This witness had told the truth. He hadn't repeated any of the rumors that were circulating about me or the lies that the investigators had suggested to him to incriminate me. I learned later that the Intelligence services had given clear instructions to the civilian witnesses. The following witness also swore to tell the truth, but I didn't think I had anything to fear from him, as he was just an ordinary client of the cybercafé. I must have crossed paths with him at the café, but we didn't know each other at all. By what magical thinking could his testimony be allowed in court?

The judge asked him:

"Does the Facebook page 'Ana Allah' belong to Waleed?"

"Yes."

"Did you see him consult the page and post articles on it?"

"Yes."

I interrupted him abruptly to ask:

"When and where did you see me? I remind you that you are under oath. What did I write there?"

Keeping to the script he had from Intelligence, he answered me:

"I saw you at the cybercafé. I didn't have to be seated immediately next to you to know what you were writing, but I know that you did."

The judge interrupted to stop us from addressing each other directly, then continued his questioning:

"Does the Facebook account also belong to Waleed?"

"Yes, it's his, registered in his name."

"Did you see him post articles there?"

"No."

Next, it was my turn to ask the witness questions:

"You said the Facebook page belongs to me and is registered under my name. How did you come to know all these details?"

"That's what people say."

"In other words, you have no proof?"

"No."

"So, if I understand correctly, you are just spreading rumors? Tell the truth: you never saw me write anything. I don't know you, we've never met."

"Yes, we have! We were at the cybercafé at the same time, four or five times. You didn't notice me, but I was watching you."

"So, we were in the same place at the same time, but we never spoke. That's hardly enough to testify against me in a case you know absolutely nothing about."

Losing patience, I began shouting at the judge:

"Are all your witnesses like this? Since when does the court allow witnesses who just repeat what the authorities want to hear? How low will the Palestinian justice system stoop? You break the law by calling a member of the military to testify against a civilian, and your other witness doesn't even know me. This trial is a farce, where the courtroom is the set and the story has already been written. I want to know the truth."

"I won't allow you to criticize this court," the judge retorted. "You have already blasphemed Allah, his Prophet, and Islam."

"No, I never insulted God, the Prophet, or Islam. All I have done is describe what I see and what I understand."

"My role is to listen to testimony, not be put on trial myself. That's the last time I will tolerate such an outburst. If you do it again, I will suspend the trial."

The judge called a fourth witness to the stand, but no one came forward. It was the prosecutor who had escorted me to the medical exam the day of my arrest. After waiting a full hour for him to arrive, the judge adjourned the court for two weeks. In other words, I had another long wait ahead, back in my jail cell.

Two days later, the director of Intelligence called me into his office, where some municipal dignitaries were waiting for me: the deputy to the Palestinian legislative council and the local Fatah official. They were typical elected officials: uneducated and owing their seats to their family ties or some past militant activities, which might even have earned them some time in an Israeli jail. Our elected officials are chosen neither on the basis of their merits nor on their political or social platform, so why would they ever feel a duty to represent the people, with all the responsibility that entails?

I had not even taken a seat before the Fatah official began berating me:

"How dare you say that you are Allah? Have you lost your mind? Are you crazy? It's unacceptable! Aren't you afraid of God and the punishment that awaits you when you die? Don't you know God will turn you into an animal? You are from a good family with a good education. How could you do this?"

"I never claimed to be Allah. That's just what people say. You shouldn't listen to rumors. And I'm not afraid of being changed into an animal; that's just a legend. Where is the girl who became a monkey because she loved music better than her prayers? There are plenty of stories like that, but there is no truth to any of them. Imams continue to call Jews monkeys and pigs because that's what the Prophet called them when they refused to convert to Islam. If I'm well educated, maybe that's what has allowed me to think for myself."

"So, everyone is a liar, and only you know the truth? Since you say you're Allah, why don't you save yourself and walk out of this jail?"

"I never pretended I was God. Let me remind you that your own beliefs say that Allah is so powerful he doesn't need your help or anyone else's to defend himself or punish me. In any case, the God you imagine is only an idea, and ideas don't need to be proven, isn't that so?"

"In the name of God the Merciful!" he exclaimed. "Will you persist in your atheism? I hope they give you the heaviest sentence possible. You are a *kafir*, an unbeliever."

After our heated exchange, the deputy, who was from my own family, intervened to say something to the Fatah official:

"Don't be so hard on him. Waleed has read too much. He has been led astray by Western culture, but he will return to the path of Islam. I know him. Our job is to help him see the error of his ways, rather than frighten him."

He turned to me next:

"Don't worry. We'll find a solution to your problem."

"What solution would that be? The judge has suspended the trial until the prosecutor can testify, and I'm still in jail."

I was summoned the following night to the investigator's office.

"How are you?"

"I feel helpless and lost. I don't know where this is going or what to expect."

"I understand, but I have some advice for you and I hope you will take it to heart. Stop discussing religious questions. Say that you lost your way in your adolescence and that you were just rebelling. Let everyone know that you are going to wake up and come back to Islam. It's the only way you are going to be released. I want what's best for you; believe me. I've come to know you, and I understand you. I'm speaking to you as a friend. I'm going to tell everyone, here and elsewhere, that you are planning on returning to the faith and asking God for forgiveness and his mercy. I'm going to do this to help you, and I hope that you will cooperate."

I could see that he meant what he said, and I thanked him for his advice and for his concern for me. I returned to my cell, ruminating what I had just heard. I had to admit I couldn't keep up the fight forever. I couldn't keep swimming against the current.

Since nothing connected me to the culture of the people around me — or rather their lack of culture — or their customs, I decided to play the game for a while. I was too sincere in my beliefs to return to Islam or to pretend to, but I decided to follow the example of the reed that bends but never breaks or the water that finds its way around the rocks to continue down the river. In other words, I would show a little more flexibility from now on.

The following morning, the director of Intelligence sent for me.

"I have heard that you are feeling better and that you are even thinking of repenting and returning to Islam?"

"I think many things, and it's always possible I might rethink my way of seeing the world. I'm looking for the truth, that's all. You know that."

"I hope you succeed. However, I wanted to see you about a different matter. You are going to be moved to a prison. This is only a detention center here; not a penitentiary."

"I won't go. You cannot lock me up with thieves and drug dealers and all sorts of criminals. I'm not like them. That's the worst thing that could happen to me. Prisons are violent places where I'll have to fight for my life all the time or be murdered. You always said I had to stay here because this was the only place where I was safe, and now you are going to put me in prison? If there's no other option, I'd rather be released and risk being murdered in the street than be locked up with criminals."

"So you won't go?"

"No, I refuse."

He wrote up a statement for me to sign to make my request official, then sent me back to my cell. Had I done the right thing? The weeks went by, monotonously. The only activity was my parents' weekly visits and my repeated demands to be released, which were systematically rejected by the judge. My trial was postponed indefinitely until the prosecutor could testify.

Things got worse once Ramadan began: I could no longer eat, drink, or smoke.

Fortunately, during the second week, the guard on duty was the friendly one, and he wasn't observing Ramadan. We shared his food, and he lent me a lighter, which I hid so as to smoke in secret.

The third week was grueling. Back in court, the prosecutor was still absent, and the judge announced my trial would be postponed again. I could hold back my frustration no longer and demanded to know what kind of a justice system could not even summon a witness on the orders of the Security services. The judge paid no attention to me and adjourned the trial for a month until after Eid al-Fitr. He ordered me transferred back to the detention center, but he also announced that my request to be released would be examined that same afternoon.

I lost my composure and cursed the Palestinian Authority and its justice system and said many other things, unable anymore to control my anger. It was inconceivable to me that I was going to have to spend another month in detention: my eleventh. I had been deprived of my freedom for far too long already. I couldn't imagine my family celebrating Eid without me. Even if I wasn't a Muslim anymore, I enjoyed spending the holidays with friends and family. Back in jail, I could see no hope for my case. My cell seemed like a tomb, and I felt as if I was being suffocated. I was in shock, under stress, depressed, and angry. My life flashed before my eyes as if I were dying, and it became crystal clear to me that religious oppression, persecution, and indoctrination will never be stronger than people's curiosity and hunger to learn. Religious leaders spread their ignorant ideas to keep their flock in line, but sometimes someone can see their lies for what they are.

I had created my blog and written articles in defense of free and open expression to counter the obscurantism that is covering our societies in a blanket of ignorance. I wanted to be that voice of rebellion that breaks the silence imposed by tyrants: the voice of reason that rings high and clear even though it has been trampled by fundamentalists. I wanted ideas to circulate freely in our societies, where religious teaching is doing all it can to strangle them.

The guard interrupted my thoughts: the director of Intelligence wanted to see me again. I was taken back to his office, not knowing whether I was in for more questioning, another conversation, or a surprise visit.

When I arrived, he indicated I should sit down and began to speak:

"How are you feeling?"

"Not well at all. I can't take this any longer."

"I have some good news for you."

"The day has been eventful enough already, " I said sarcastically.

"The judge has granted your release."

"I don't believe it! Is this another trick to weaken my resolve?"

"No, it's the truth," he said, showing me the signed release form.

I couldn't contain my joy. I was ecstatic at the idea of being a free man again and being able to return to my family and friends, after ten months of illegal detention. I was also proud that I had never weakened and had remained true to myself until the very end.

I asked him for the date of my release. He explained that he had sent the paperwork to the central administration office and that he was waiting for them to officialize it, which usually took about three days. I thanked him and returned to my cell.

I didn't sleep at all that night. I began planning my return in my mind, imagining what it would be like to see my brothers and sisters again after ten months. I dreamed again, about how I could change society and save it from its ignorance, defending human rights and the cause of the oppressed and minorities.

For the next two days, I wasn't allowed to speak to anyone. This silence was menacing: fear and doubt began to nag at me again. Had my request for release been revoked? Had the administrative authorities blocked it? I asked to see the investigator, who had me brought to his office.

"We are waiting for the response from Security headquarters," he said.

"But, you said that they had no more oversight of my case, once it had been transferred to the court. Now that the court has given the go-ahead, are you blocking the decision?"

"No. Once the court makes its decision, which is usually enforceable, Security still has to approve it. Normally, there's no problem. Stop worrying and be patient a day or two more."

"Thanks."

"I want to ask you a question: do you ever have nightmares?"

"No, never. You've already asked me that. Why would I?"

"The fear of God and of Hell!"

"How can I be afraid of something that doesn't exist? God is only an abstraction, and there's nothing frightening about that. Atheists who have

nightmares aren't truly convinced of their beliefs; it's their doubt and fear
of God that makes them dream."

On the second day, with Eid approaching, the director of Intelligence
summoned me. I found him in his office with both the investigator and
the prosecutor. Both were looking daggers at me.

The director of Intelligence broke the silence:

"Today, you will return home, and tonight you will sleep in your own
bed. You'll see your parents, your brothers, your sisters. But, before leaving here, there are a few formalities to address. First of all, you must
swear to never let it be known that you were tortured or subjected to any
kind of psychological intimidation here. If you do, you will be arrested
immediately."

"I agree. I just want to go home."

"You will have to sign a paper saying you will never repeat your crimes
or publish your writings. Your phone and Internet use will be under surveillance. You are forbidden from contacting anyone outside of your family. You will have to appear once a day at police headquarters. You may
not leave the country. You will have to be present at all hearings for the
duration of your trial. You will always say that you were treated well by
Intelligence services and that you were never deprived of food or water."

"I agree."

"You will never speak of your detention here, not even in ten or
twenty years. Everything you saw and heard here stays here."

"I agree."

"Now, you are going to follow the investigator back to his office, where
you will sign the documents. Your father must sign them, as well."

My father was waiting in the investigator's office. I signed a single
page notifying me of my release. My father had to sign a stack of documents and promise to see that I would never publish any of my articles
nor engage in deviant activities. He also had to agree to accompany me
to the courthouse at every summons and watch over me so that I might
return to the faith. If he failed to fulfill any of these conditions, he could
be imprisoned and heavily fined. Finally, he signed a paper stating that he
found me in good health with no signs of ill treatment.

Before leaving, I asked for my cell phone. The investigator didn't know where it was but thought that it was probably at the courthouse, in which case I would have to wait until the end of the trial to get it back. I took my belongings and ran to my father's car. I had ten months of life to catch up.

Chapter IV
Freedom!

A round ten o'clock at night, my father and I were in his car on the way to the house. As we drove, he explained to me that the director of Intelligence had summoned him by phone while he was at the barbershop. He had been working late because he had so many clients in the days leading up to Eid. He had come directly from the shop to take care of the paperwork and bring me home. No one else in my family knew.

I will never forget the date: September 3, 2011. That was the day I saw my family again after ten months of detention. My father dropped me off: he had to go straight back to the barbershop. I opened the door and stopped in the entrance hall a long moment, breathing in the smell of my family home and all of my childhood. I ran my hand over the walls; I wanted to kiss them. My ten months of detention had felt like an eternity. My heart began to race as I climbed the stairs.

I opened the door of the living room, where my mother, my brothers, and sisters were watching television. I threw my arms open wide and shouted: "I am free!" Until my dying day, I will never forget the image of my mother, overcome with joy and calling out my name: "Waleeeeeed!" She ran to me and hugged me tightly to her, my brothers and sisters followed, and I collapsed onto the floor under them.

My mother hastily made dinner and a fresh fruit juice, and I spent the entire night—right until *suhur*, which is the predawn meal before a day of fasting during Ramadan—telling them everything that had happened over the previous ten months. My mother spread the news of my return to our closest friends, and they promised to come to the house after Eid. At dawn, I ate *suhur* with my family and decided to sleep all day to respect their fasting. It was the last day of Ramadan; it wasn't too much to ask.

On the day of Eid, the house filled with visitors. Friends, neighbors, and relatives came to extend their best wishes for the feast day while using the occasion to celebrate my release and ask about my plans. I told them I would have to wait until the end of the trial, set for the following month, before making any decisions.

After Eid was over, I began to leave the house, always with one of my brothers or a close friend or relation. I was anxious to see how people who disapproved of me would react. Passersby in the street called me the *kafir*—unbeliever—but were not aggressive, limiting themselves to probing looks, whispers, and questions about my release. Everyone seemed convinced by the rumor that I was a paid agent of the West; my release, after all, was proof enough for them. The rumor had been spread by certain members of my extended family, in particular by a first cousin in the Liberation Party, a radical Islamist movement hoping for the return of the Caliphate, who was spreading lies about me to the public. Another cousin, a former deputy and a member of Hamas, gave my parents the cold shoulder because of their "renegade son." Some friends had cut all ties with my family. Professors and students at the university put heightened pressure on my sisters, calling them "sisters of the unbeliever." Certain female teachers who were members of Hamas insulted them constantly because of me. How many times had my brothers been heckled into a fight with a stranger because of my convictions? My brothers were the youngest in the family, however, and didn't share the ideas of their oldest sibling; on the contrary, they kept a safe distance from my beliefs. But their refusal to banish me from the family made them guilty in the eyes of everyone else. My mother was frequently reduced to tears by the impolite looks and hateful comments of certain friends. It was unbearable: I couldn't go out alone anywhere, especially not at night. Fanatics were too numerous to count, and their hatred, combined with rumors and fatwas, made it too dangerous for me to go out alone.

My hopes for living a normal life had vanished. After only a week of freedom, I realized that I was completely isolated from this backward and incurably ill society that had rejected me for sharing my opinions, while it continued to tolerate criminals, rapists, and thieves. Our intellectual, cultural, and religious incompatibility was complete and total. Even people who were close to me began avoiding me, stricken by that illness that transforms men into unthinking sheep.

After long reflection, I decided that my avoidance of others was a sign of weakness: I had to take the bull by the horns and break my silence. It would be far better to defend myself in a debate than be the victim of rumors.

The conditions of my release were clear, however; while awaiting my trial, I had to check in daily at police headquarters and I couldn't leave the city or use the phone or Internet. To pass the time and make myself useful, I helped my father in his barbershop until, one day, two plain clothes officers came in. They introduced themselves as Military Intelligence agents and escorted me without further explanation to the director of this latest Security service. I was immediately ushered into his office.

"When were you released from detention?"

"Two weeks ago. I'm under house arrest, I have no means of communication, and I must appear at the police station every day."

"Do you know why you were brought in?"

"No."

"There is a blasphemous Facebook page called "Allah." We think you are the author."

"I'm not allowed to use a computer. Are you going to accuse me every time an article criticizing Islam appears on the Internet?"

He turned his computer screen to face me so I could see the page.

"This isn't recent; it was published while I was in jail. How could I be the author?"

"You're right. We received orders from Ramallah to arrest you. I'm going to find out why."

The officer called the Palestinian Authority in Ramallah, and the conversation was intense. The officer wanted to know why he had received orders to arrest me when there was no justifiable motive. Finally, he hung up and announced that he was going to detain me until they could check if I was involved in any way. It was a Thursday evening. Because public offices and courts are closed Friday and Saturday, that meant I was going to be there an extra two days.

I protested this arbitrary decision, reminding them it would interfere with my daily obligation to check in with the police. It was a lost cause: I would be held at the jail at police headquarters. I was terrified by the idea of being locked up with all kinds of criminals who might want to kill me. The officer was reassuring: "You'll be with juvenile delinquents who won't be interested in you."

During the car ride to the jail, I thought about everything that had happened during the previous ten months, my imprisonment, torture, and psychological intimidation. How much longer could this punishment last? My feeling of freedom, so recent, was also so fragile. I worried about how my cellmates would react to seeing me there, about what my parents and neighbors would think. People's hatred only needed a spark to flare up again.

I was put in a damp cell that stunk of mold, with insects crawling all over the walls. The extremely poor conditions didn't prevent the four other men in the cell from sleeping soundly, however. As for myself, the fear of being assaulted kept me awake all night. As day began to break, I started a conversation with an older man, who didn't look anything like a criminal, and who shared the cell with three adolescents. After the usual salutations, he recognized me but said that only God could judge me. He then began to tell me his story, after four months of total silence since his arrest. He explained that the court summoned him once a month, only to postpone the trial every time and reject all of his requests for release or parole. His case was so unusual, you could either laugh or cry listening to it. He told me:

"I'm a pious man, simple and poor. I was working 12 hours a day as a shop clerk to support my family. One day, I refused to serve a man who was angry and aggressive and who had insulted me. Exasperated, I insulted him back. This man worked for the infamous Preventive Security. He arrested me. That was four months ago."

His story deeply upset me. His family had only been able to visit him once because they lived outside of the city and had no means of transportation to come into the city. But he preferred it that way, as it spared them that ordeal and allowed him to keep his sense of dignity; he couldn't bear them seeing him in his current state of acute distress.

I was struck by the injustice of his story. Citizens, if they can even be called that in my country, have no value whatsoever, I thought. When force substitutes for law, Palestinians have no choice but to give up hope. How many innocent people like this man were rotting in prison?

When I told him the reasons for my arrest, he grinned a wide smile:

"I insulted a Preventive Security agent and I have been in jail for four months. You insulted the Prophet: I can't dare imagine how long you'll be in here for."

We burst out in wild laughter, which eased the tension in the cell. The three adolescents were surprised to see the older man talking to me. He was suspicious of them, for fear they were agents, too, while in reality they had only stolen a farmer's crops to sell them at market.

When my detention was over, I was taken to see the director of Military Intelligence, who told me I was free to go since no evidence against me had been found. However, he warned me:

"If you make the slightest error, or criticize the Prophet one more time, I promise you I will be the first one to kill you, to avenge and protect Islam. Are you a blogger?"

"I was. Not any longer."

"Bloggers are deviants, all of them. Some of them expose themselves on Internet; others blaspheme Islam. They are manipulated by Zionists and Freemasons."

"But there is nowhere where people who don't share your ideas can go to speak freely, without fear of censure."

"Say whatever you like; it's no concern of mine. In the meantime, I have confiscated your computer to see what is on it. We will return it tomorrow or the day after. Now you'll have to wait for your father to arrive; he will take you home."

At home, my mother welcomed me with a large smile, her way of letting me know that my second arrest was meaningless to her. She tried to reassure me, saying I wasn't responsible for everything that circulates on the Internet and convinced that the authorities would eventually forget me. I got my computer back two days later, but it didn't work anymore. Was it the result of incompetence or sabotage? In any case, even after it was repaired, all my archived data were lost.

My arrest had started the rumor mill up again. People in my neighborhood and in the city were saying that I had resumed my former activities on Facebook. My cousin who was close to an Islamist movement was telling people I was still locked up. Exasperated, my father asked me to put an end to all the talk. I thought he'd never ask.

The first chance we had, my brother and I went to where my cousin worked. We waited until he was alone to burst into his office.

"Here I am! I'm free. I'm not in jail. Take a good look at me and from now on stop talking about me."

"My dear cousin, I was worried, that's all," he retorted.

"Worry doesn't justify the rumors you are spreading about me all over town. You only had to go see my father at his barbershop, which is next to your house, to find out how I am. It's your terrorist movement that pretends to defend Islam that is encouraging you to mobilize public opinion against me and against the Palestinian Authority that freed me. But all that is over. Do you understand me?"

The path back to a normal life was going to be a long one, with many obstacles, mostly religious ones.

My sister Wafaa was engaged to be married. As is customary, the young man's family had inquired about ours before formally asking for Wafaa's hand, and my father had looked into theirs, as well, before accepting. After so many months of anguish, my family desperately needed a reason to be happy, if only for a moment. I was supposed to be a witness to the ceremony but the imam wouldn't allow me to sign the marriage register, on the grounds that I was an unbeliever.

The celebrations were over quickly, and the following day I was summoned again by Military Intelligence: my articles were still available on the Internet.

"You must erase all the articles that carry your signature."

"Some of those articles are over five years old and have been republished on sites that I know nothing about. My blog was shut down, and I don't have the password anymore."

"That's your problem. You'll stay in detention until everything is gone."

Like the previous time, my arrest had been ordered on a Thursday, and I was transferred to the same cell where I found my old friend and two new prisoners wearing beards: a sixty-year-old imam and a young man in his thirties. With an ironic smile on his face, the old man welcomed me back and invited me to take "my reserved seat" amongst them. The three thieves had been released, but the man, who had only been goaded by the insults of a Preventive Security agent, was still there. The two new prisoners recognized me immediately and began asking God for forgiveness. They requested a transfer to a different cell, under the pretext that their religion forbade them from sharing a room and food with an unbeliever. Their request was rejected. Since we were going to have to live together, I decided to confront them with their own weapons:

"Instead of asking for a new cell, why don't you try to convert me back to Islam? Your place in Paradise would be guaranteed, and the sins that have led to your arrest would be forgiven."

"We aren't here to preach. We have other worries before our trial."

"If you went about it right, maybe I could be convinced to come back to the faith."

One of them, the imam, then began to tell me about himself.

I learned that he was about sixty years old and had three wives. They seemed to tolerate the situation and even encourage it, since they had gone with him when he asked for a fourth wife in marriage. It wasn't surprising that his wives, in their submissive role as sex objects, had accompanied him; they were raised in those beliefs and behaviors. What disgusted me was that his fourth wife was only 14 years old and could have been his granddaughter.

The Quran authorizes this practice; the example was set by the Prophet and the young Aisha, who was only nine years old when he married her. In Palestine even today, young girls are found dead the day after their weddings, literally ripped open by their husbands' sexual furor. Beyond their physical incompatibility—an adult penis penetrating a child's body—religious leaders are unconcerned by the psychological trauma endured by these young girls if they survive. Suddenly cut off from their families, their adolescence abruptly terminated, they generally suffer from severe psychological disorders. With no knowledge of what a proper conjugal relationship should be and unprepared for the responsibilities of keeping house and raising children, they become seriously depressed.

These marriages are arranged for financial motives only and are very common in Arab countries. Fathers sell their daughters to their future sons-in-law, who are ready to pay a generous price for a beauty. Contemporary legislation would treat an arrangement of this sort as illegal human trafficking and disguised prostitution. Men who look to marry a girl don't do so to create a family and build a home with someone who is still a child herself; their intention is to enjoy the sexual pleasure that these young female bodies can give them. These girls are still too young to understand what it is to be a wife and a mother. I am opposed to the forced marriage of girls as well as any traditional marriage whose objective is to satisfy a man's libido and give him children, with no thought for love or for family. Very often in traditional marriages, husband and wife hardly know each other, and there is no bond between them. Their union is a simple "transaction." The girls, who must of course be virgins, are judged for their "market value," determined by their beauty, modesty, and other attractive features. Future mothers-in-law go looking for the prettiest girls and then make inquiries regarding their qualities and their family status before "reserving" them for their sons. Whether the girls are educated or cultured means nothing; the most important thing is that they are virgins, untouched by any man, and the youngest are the most valuable. Negotiations with the girl's family revolve around the amount of the bride price, with the prettiest fetching the highest amounts. The father pockets the money and hands over his daughter, who becomes the property of her husband. She has no rights and can never ask for a divorce: she is a victim, pure and simple. These oppressive traditions that come straight from our tribal, patriarchal past perpetuate the idea of female inferiority and keep women in a state of submission. These practices must be stopped immediately, as they are an outrage to contemporary principles of equality and freedom and, moreover, encourage fathers, brothers, uncles, and cousins to commit so-called honor crimes when the women in their families are accused of having extramarital relations with a man. So many innocent girls are murdered to "wash the honor" of their families, while their killers escape justice because their actions are condoned by society.

I was released on Sunday and returned home, wondering how I could leave the country. I asked my brother to find me an Israeli cell phone I could use to contact certain human rights organizations. I sent them all the information I had about my case, but these NGOs are not very good at anything other than promoting themselves through media campaigns.

Three months went by, during which I spent about ten weekends in jail, arrested always on a Thursday and released on a Sunday. I heard nothing from the NGOs. Desperate, I contacted the journalist Diaa Hadid, who had reported on my case, and I granted her an interview. She agreed to wait for my green light to publish it. The moment had arrived.

I decided to leave the country for which I had given everything of myself: my blood, tears, love, dreams, and hopes. In return, my country wanted to take away my freedom, my dignity, and my convictions. I rejected my country, just like I had rejected Islam. Muslims may celebrate all they want, but I refused to stay in any country that disrespects intellectuals, humiliates scientists, and forbids love. I chose to go far from the Arab world and Islam to somewhere I could finally live as a free man.

I thought about crossing into Israel, but it was too risky. Thanks to a bilateral agreement with the Palestinian Authority, the Israelis could arrest me and extradite me to the West Bank. Taking that route would also unleash a new round of rumors accusing me of working for Zionists to overthrow Islam. I contacted some Western embassies in the West Bank to apply for a visa but found out that, for security reasons, none of them maintained a consular presence in Palestine, leaving Palestinians in the same dilemma as Iraqis and Syrians, who are forced to use consulates in Jordan to apply for foreign visas.

I had an aunt who lived and worked in Jordan. My passport allowed me to cross the border at the Israeli checkpoint. I packed a small bag, notified certain Jordanian friends, and, a few days before my departure, I told my parents of my plans. I persuaded my father and promised my mother I would return as soon as possible, but she wasn't convinced. After a long talk, she came around to my decision, or at least pretended to, but she hid my passport all the same.

With my go-ahead, the journalist Diaa Hadid published her interview with me on February 1, 2012. The article defused the situation and relieved me of the obligation of appearing at the police station every day. I still had to be present at my trial, however, scheduled for April 20.

I ordered a taxi to pick me up at dawn on February 14, 2012. On Valentine's Day, that symbolic holiday celebrating love, I left a country riven by hatred and driven by a religion that espouses violence and discrimination, when all I wanted was to see it live in a spirit of solidarity and equality.

I had spent the preceding evening with my parents, my aunt who lived with us, my brothers, and my sisters. We all cried over this forced separation, but they were generous with their advice and encouragement. It was a sad night. None of us wanted me to leave, but exile was my only solution.

The taxi arrived at four o'clock in the morning. The driver was a close friend of my father's with no affection for either the Palestinian Authority or the Islamists. I couldn't hold back my tears; I was leaving my family and my country, and I was certain I would never return. I would always be persecuted in a society that wants nothing more than to tear everything and everyone apart.

I hugged my brothers, my sisters, my father, and my aunt before finally embracing my mother. "Darling, don't wait long to come back," she murmured, her voice breaking with emotion. Her words veiled just barely what she knew in her heart and what she hoped despite it all. On the one hand, she knew there was no place for me in Palestinian society; on the other, she remained hopeful something would change. Her words were barely audible, but they still ring in my ears, overwhelming me with sadness.

Through the taxi window, I watched as the places of my childhood flashed by: the school, the park where I used to play with my schoolmates, friends' houses, the forest where I smoked my first cigarette, and, finally, Security headquarters: so many symbolic stops on the road to freedom.

At the border near Jericho, the taxi driver dropped me off at the checkpoint and wished me luck. I showed my passport to the Israeli soldiers and paid the entrance fee, then waited for over an hour while they verified I wasn't wanted for terrorist activities in Israel. I took a shuttle to the Jordanian checkpoint, then a bus to Amman. My parents phoned me regularly to reassure themselves that I had not encountered any problems along the way and to remind me that my aunt was waiting for me in Amman.

My aunt was a recently retired school teacher and had been a widow for several years. She had raised her five children alone, giving them her strong personality and encouraging them to pursue their studies at university. The youngest was my age and shared his room with me. He also managed a cybercafé, which made things much easier for me.

That night at dinner, I recounted in detail what had happened to me over the past year and confided that I hoped to obtain political asylum in the United States in order to continue my fight.

In my cousin's cybercafé, I was finally able to connect to the Internet. I only had to type my name into any Arab-language search engine to find thousands of articles, 95 percent of which were critical of me. I had seen it all before: I was a traitor, an unbeliever; I was crazy, I was mentally ill. I was the mastermind of an international network plotting to destroy Islam. Even if the opinions of these bloggers were not entirely identical, they all agreed I should be assassinated. For some, the worst thing I had done was to refuse their mass-produced culture that produces nothing better than beggars and unemployed legions of backwards, brainwashed failures in life. Others criticized me for having wanted to live in a free, cultivated world, for vaunting the merits of freedom and equality and for exposing their hypocrisy. Still others didn't like that I had thought for myself and espoused humanistic values that ran counter to theirs and that I had publicly denounced their ideology and wanted others to share my ideas.

Radical Islam imposes its own rules on society, rejects any opposition, challenges anyone who wants to live independently, excludes any other philosophy, and executes the "infidels." I had refused to listen to religious leaders and to give credence to their lies and barbarous actions. That was enough for them to declare war on me. The really indoctrinated ones wanted to kill me, hoping to reserve their place in Paradise and avoid the eternal fires of Hell. The few articles describing the best methods for executing me, although distressing to read at times, proved nevertheless that they were specialists at killing.

The remaining 5 percent of articles published about me in Arabic defended me and demanded my release. Reports by NGOs and certain Facebook pages criticized my arbitrary arrest and accused the Palestinian authority of violating universal human rights. My former students had also mobilized in my defense, though I had been their teacher for just six months. On online forums, I read: "Waleed was the best teacher. The authorities are lying just to incriminate him." I was proud of the work I had done with them; I had helped these young people to learn to think for themselves, using their intelligence only, in a society where everything is explained by divine legend.

I also learned that the French government had officially asked the Palestinian Authority to release me, as my safety could not be guaranteed otherwise. Michèle Alliot-Marie herself, the Minister of Defense, had interceded on my behalf. France's support was encouraging: why not request political asylum in France? I didn't know anyone there, however, and didn't speak the language. I decided to keep looking for a solution elsewhere.

On English-language sites, I read hundreds of articles defending me and demanding my release and worrying about the Palestinian Authority's radicalization. I came across my blog, also, and I was sickened to see that the only thing left on it was a statement by the Palestinian Authority, in my name, excusing myself and asking for forgiveness for having blasphemed Islam. Five years of work and over two million visitors had vanished.

I also found my Facebook page, "I'm Proud to Be An Atheist." The number of subscribers had literally exploded since my arrest.

I reactivated my Facebook accounts and contacted my friends in Jordan and elsewhere, giving them my new phone number.

I printed out a selection of articles to justify my applications for visas to Western countries. Canada was my first choice; I had a friend there who was willing to let me stay with her and who had written an official letter of invitation. There was an unusual snowstorm in Jordan that paralyzed the country and slowed my plans by a week, but the delay allowed me to spend time with my closest friends there, Ahmed al-Jaafra and Samir Kassab, true brothers to me.

I was refused a Canadian tourist visa on the grounds that I had never traveled abroad and that my request might be hiding a plan to immigrate permanently. After a few failed attempts to find a solution through a variety of specialized organizations like the United Nations Relief and Works Agency, I decided to leave Amman and travel to Zarqa, about 13 miles away, where I had a second aunt. Her son welcomed me enthusiastically:

"I am proud of you and what you are doing. I think you are the best thing my family and Palestine have produced," he said to comfort me.

He was a gynecologist and knew many people. He introduced me to a friend who suggested I enroll at a university in a Western country for a student visa. If all else failed, I could always try my chances with the clandestine immigration networks that operated by boat. Neither of these propositions was appealing. It would take too long to apply to a university, and my trial date was looming. In the meantime, the Jordanian authorities could arrest me, and the Palestinian Authority could ask for my extradition to the West Bank, which would complicate my case. Finally, I refused the indignity of the clandestine route.

My mother called me daily to tell me about the preparations for my other sister's wedding. She hoped I would return to Qalqilya for it, since I was still waiting for a visa. Unfortunately, another aunt passed away a few days later, and the wedding was postponed for forty days, until after the traditional mourning period.

While I was waiting to leave Amman, I rented an apartment, which took the burden of housing me off my aunt and gave me more freedom. I telephoned the French embassy and explained my case briefly to the director of communications. Her name was Clémence, and she gave me an appointment for the following day to provide more details. When I arrived, she greeted me with a large smile and looked at all the documents I brought.

"What would you like the embassy and France to do for you?" she asked, when she had finished examining my papers.

"I would like them to grant me asylum and protection."

"I will see what we can do. Once your file is complete, I'll send your request to Paris by diplomatic pouch. We'll have an answer in three days."

"I would be so grateful to you. My life is truly in danger, and I can't stay much longer in Jordan. My trial date is April 20."

"I'll do what's needed and keep you posted."

A few days later, I still had no news and was extremely worried. I called Clémence, who put my fears to rest:

"Your file is complete and has already been sent to Paris."

The following Thursday, she told me that my request had been accepted and gave me an appointment at the embassy to complete the remaining formalities, one of which was to provide an address in France. She reassured me that a hotel address would suffice.

I was giddy with joy and my head was spinning; I thought I must be dreaming. After I calmed down, I decided to keep quiet about my news for a little while longer, since I still didn't have any concrete proof. I logged into my Facebook account, however, to ask my contacts for an address in Paris. One of my friends, Qassem al-Ghazali, suggested I contact Randa Kassis, a secular member of the Syrian opposition based in Paris, a formidable personality and an exceptional individual. I phoned her, and she offered me her support immediately:

"Don't worry; I'll help you," she told me.

I appeared at the French embassy the following Sunday for my appointment, carrying a Paris address. A few minutes later, I was leaving again, with my type D, three-month visa. I would find out later that it would allow me to obtain a residency card and a work permit in France, as long as I filed a request within the first two months following my arrival in France.

There are two dates that stand out for me: September 3, 2011, the day of my release, and the Sunday I received my visa to travel to France. I shared my news with my friends, Ahmed and Samir, and with my aunt, of course. Everyone congratulated me and wished me luck in my new life. Would I have ever found a way out without my guardian angel Clémence and her invaluable help? I telephoned my cousin at the cybercafé to ask him to send a copy of my visa to my parents. He told me to meet him at his mother's house. Some of the clients at the cybercafé had recognized me and were accusing me of having written a blasphemous Quran. They were very agitated and angry at me.

When we met a little while later, he explained what had happened: a Jordanian website had announced I was in Amman and had published photos of me, as well. My life was in danger, not just in the West Bank and in Jordan but in every country under Muslim rule! I reserved a flight to Paris leaving April 2, 2012. I would have to wait a week, during which I hoped to see my friends, for the last time perhaps, and celebrate my freedom with them. After having spent six weeks in Jordan, I thought of them already as brothers; their support knew no bounds. Now that I had been discovered, however, I would have to be careful.

My father and my aunt wired money to me, to help pay for my plane ticket and whatever costs I would have until I could get settled in Paris. The day before my departure, my friends organized a barbecue to send me off. It was a fabulous evening. Ahmed stayed so he could drop me at the Amman Queen Alia International Airport the following day.

At the ticket counter, the agent informed me that my papers were not in order. I immediately suspected the worst: an arrest warrant from the Palestinian Authority. The situation was much simpler, however; the police officer explained that my Jordanian visa had expired two weeks prior and that I would need to pay a fine of ten Jordanian dinars (approximately fifteen dollars). It looked to me more like a simple bribe than an actual fine, but I paid him with a smile.

To my great surprise, at the gate, I ran into the Palestinian Security officer who had led the investigation for the Intelligence services and who had spent so many hours in discussion with me. It could have been a scene from a movie: two men who had met in prison, from different sides of the bars of a cell, meet again in happier circumstances.

"Waleed? What are you doing here?"

"I could ask you the same question."

"I was in Egypt for medical reasons and I'm just returning. What about you?"

"I've been granted asylum in France, and I'm boarding a flight to Paris in an hour."

"That's the best thing that could have happened to you. There is no future for you in Palestine."

"But how will my trial go? It's due to start in a few days."

"I have no idea. They'll close your case, one way or the other."

"That would also be the best outcome for everyone."

"You know, Waleed, I was under orders from my superiors. I authorized your parents to bring you food and I advised you to avoid debating questions of religion with strangers, to help you avoid useless trouble. After reading your articles and talking with you, I am certain you are an educated and cultivated man, but I can't tolerate your saying God doesn't exist."

"I understand."

"I have to tell you that you opened certain people's eyes and roiled some stagnant waters."

"In the beginning, it's true, I just wanted to stir things up and make people think. But now I want to do more: I want to help society enter the modern world and put an end to its obscurantism."

"You're young still, with plenty of time ahead of you. Yours is the Internet generation, and like all young people, you're in a hurry. You want

everything to change right away. Things aren't so simple, however. What
fascinates me about you is your determination and your strategy. You have
both feet planted firmly on the ground; I know you'll go far."

"You're undoubtedly right; I learned that you have to study societal
behaviors to understand, anticipate, and accompany their evolution. The
society I belong to is Muslim, but I am not a Muslim, and when you know
that God doesn't exist and Superman can't do anything to help you, you
can only count on yourself."

"Palestinians' are nearsighted when it comes to politics, but you see
a bigger picture."

"To say the least! Palestinians only know how to follow the herd. When
there's a soccer match, everyone is a sports commentator. When there
are elections, everyone is a political scientist. But they don't understand
soccer any better than politics. For them, everything is a game that you
win by exploiting your adversary's weak spot. In the end, though, it's the
mediocrity of our leaders, whether they wear the beard or a mustache,
that creates a sterile debate that does nothing to advance society. People
make choices based on appearances, but in a modern, civilized society,
you can't judge a book by its cover!"

"I admire your courage. Watch yourself. Fundamentalists are every-
where and they are dangerous."

"I know; radical Islam is at the root of this evil and must be stopped."

"My plane is going to board soon. I have to leave. Be careful."

"Thanks."

Our conversation galvanized me. When I got on the plane that would
take me to France, I was more determined than ever to continue the fight.

Chapter V
My Kind of Freedom

In four hours I would be landing in Paris, the most beautiful city in the world, the City of Light, the capital of love. I was nervous about what it would be like for me there. I didn't have much money and I didn't speak the language or know anyone at all. Would I end up alone, sleeping under a bridge? Compared to persecution and death threats at home, however, exile and solitude in France were preferable by far.

Every immigrant sees the West as an Eldorado where life is better. I had had some time to educate myself about this "paradise," and I knew that misery was not unique to Muslim societies. What worried me the most was the unknown.

For the entire four hours of the flight, I tried to imagine myself living in Paris, conjuring up all the possible scenarios. If France rejected my asylum demand, I had cousins in Italy or I could immigrate to the United States. If Paris did grant me asylum status, how would I live? I could continue my studies and learn French, but I could also continue to militate against all forms of oppression in the Muslim world by fighting for peace and for individual rights and freedoms.

When I got off the plane, I followed the other passengers without knowing where I was going. It was my first trip, and I had never seen such an enormous airport. Instinctively, I lined up at Immigration. The police officer checked my visa and motioned me through. I picked up my bag like everyone else and then found a public telephone, where I called Randa Kassis to let her know I had arrived. She welcomed me to France and told me to meet her in front of the Paris Opera house, where she would be waiting for me with a friend. I took a taxi. The driver was Asian and very helpful; he even showed me how to purchase credit for my cell phone before we left the airport. In Paris, I stared at everything: the buildings, the people, the clean streets, the beauty of the city, the orderliness of its citizens. It was just like I had imagined it would be.

The taxi dropped me at the Opéra. The bill was seventy euros. I paid the driver without saying a word but was surprised by the exorbitant price. At that pace, my money would not last long. Yet there I was in Paris, standing in front of the Opera house, in the most beautiful city in the world. Randa Kassis was waiting for me on the sidewalk across the street. She introduced me to her friend, the wonderful Bernard Schalscha.

They wanted to know every last detail about what had happened during the previous months. I will remain eternally grateful to Randa, who helped and advised me in so many ways. I owe her absolutely everything that I did in France. If there is a god, she is my goddess. This incredible militant for women's rights and the revolution of the Syrian people always made time for me. Her help was unconditional and unlimited, and my liberal, reformist views aligned with hers.

Randa and Bernard then showed me how to use the Paris subway. I was amazed and fascinated by the Métro, such a practical and comfortable form of transportation that anyone could ride at nominal cost, especially compared to the taxi I had just taken. We went to the Bastille quarter, where Bernard had reserved a hotel room for me for four nights until I could request accommodation through an aid association for refugees seeking asylum, called France Terre d'Asile. Bernard would prove remarkably efficient in everything, helping me with all my paperwork for the government, the police, and the different aid associations and introducing me to his friends and his fellow militants in the causes he defended.

After I was settled into my room, Randa left, promising to check in with me daily. Bernard was on his way to celebrate a Jewish friend's birthday and invited me to come with him. I told him that if they didn't mind having a Palestinian join the party, I'd be pleased to meet his friends. We spent a fantastic evening. Bernard introduced me to all the guests, and I was able to talk to them in English. He had to leave in time to catch the last subway home but was concerned I wouldn't be able to find my way back to the hotel. We had come to the party on foot, however, and I was sure I could walk back by myself.

It had been a highly emotional day. I fell asleep almost as soon as I was back in my room.

The following morning, I had breakfast in the hotel and was nearly ready to leave when I realized I had forgotten to pack my hairbrush. I went to buy one in a shop next to the hotel. Instead of the fifty cents it would have sold for in Palestine, this one cost me ten euros. I was going to need a plan for managing my money.

I found the hotel on a tourist map and traced out my walking route for the day. I went first to the Place de la Bastille, then toward the Seine, crossing to the Notre-Dame Cathedral, then back to the Louvre via the Pont des Arts, before arriving at the Champs-Elysées, the most beautiful avenue in the world. I was stunned by the beauty of Paris. Finally, I went to the Eiffel Tower, where I phoned my mother to tell her everything I had done that day, taking care to describe the size and the beauty of the city. I would have loved for her to be there with me; more than the fact that I missed her, I wanted her to live in a civilized country, surrounded by beauty. I had left Qalqilya only two months before, but I missed my family already, especially my mother. Would I ever see them again? When I thought of her, would the image in my mind always be her tearful good-bye in front of the house, the day I left?

Randa called me in the evening, and I told her about my day. She recommended some other places to visit but gave me fair warning before she hung up:

"Hurry up and see everything you want now. Life in Paris can be hectic. Pretty soon you won't have any time for tourism."

Bernard also telephoned to let me know we had an appointment the following day at France Terre d'Asile.

The next morning, Bernard accompanied me to my appointment and helped me fill out papers to make a formal request for asylum. Virginie was my initial contact there. Her professionalism and humanity were

extraordinary all through the process of submitting my request and following through with the French Office for the Protection of Refugees
and Stateless People (OFPRA). She was eventually replaced by Céline,
who was just as kind and competent. Since I had left Qalqilya, all my
French contacts had been wonderful, and I will always remember them
with affection.

With the help of France Terre d'Asile, I was granted medical cover-
age and a room in a small hotel in the 18th arrondissement. The poverty I discovered in this new neighborhood of Paris was shocking; it was
hard to believe it was even part of such a beautiful city. A general lawlessness reigned there, which seemed to be a source of pride to some of the
residents. The streets were filled with homeless people, so much so that
I would have believed anyone who tried to tell me that begging was a
profession.

I found it hard to acclimate to my new environment at first, though
language wasn't a barrier, since many people in the neighborhood
spoke Arabic. When they learned I was Palestinian, they were generally
impressed and respectful. Everyone, and Algerians especially, seemed to
think Palestinians were shouldering the burden of upholding the honor of
the entire Arab world. I wasn't happy in this neighborhood, but the prices
were far cheaper than what I had seen elsewhere in Paris, and sometimes
they were even less than at home. Given the size of my savings, it was
worth staying just for that.

After I had been in Paris two months, Bernard accompanied me to the
central prefecture to request a residency permit. My type D visa allowed
me to request one after just one month in France, without any consequences for my pending asylum status, so our visit was short. I left with
a renewable, six-month residency permit and access to government aid,
while I waited for OFPRA to decide on my request for asylum and official
status as a political refugee.

I often accompanied Bernard to his appointments and public appearances. As an activist, his principle causes were the Sudan, Darfour, and
individual and collective freedoms. Together we attended the Gay Pride

parade and a demonstration against racism and fascism, as well as a weekly sit-in for the Syrian revolution. Like all the popular uprisings of the Arab Spring, the Syrian cause had my full support, even if, by and large, the results have not lived up to expectations.

The Syrian revolution had become dangerously mired down, with hundreds of thousands dead and injured, and millions of refugees and displaced people. A popular uprising for freedom and dignity had become a complex and expensive civil war against a dictatorial regime that governed on the basis of state-supported terrorism and manipulation alone. Whole regions of the country had been destroyed and emptied of their inhabitants. The sheer number of displaced people was a burden for the opposition party's political and military leaders, as thousands were forced to abandon the revolution because they were too busy just trying to survive.

The revolt of the Syrian people against their despotic government has turned into an international conflict, with serious consequences. Islamist terrorist groups want to forcibly impose a caliphate whose laws run counter to everything the people have been demanding. Blatantly hostile to democracy, these groups have undermined the revolution and awakened fear of Syrians, whereas the relevance and the legitimacy of the Syrian revolution's initial demands should have found sympathy and support.

History reminds us that revolutions are never simple affairs. The more fiercely a despotic government clings to power, the longer the revolution takes to achieve its goals. The Syrian revolution is no exception. Nevertheless, when all peaceful and progressive means have been exhausted, revolution remains the only way to free oppressed peoples and demand change. Syrians never would have resorted to bloodshed if the regime had instituted reforms and if the president had agreed to leave power, after four decades of rule, after all. Instead, the regime shouted its message loud and clear: "Assad or the country burns" or "Assad for eternal president." Rather than began a peaceful transfer of power, Assad destroyed his country and massacred its people.

In May, Randa and Bernard gave me a one-of-a-kind experience. They were going to the Cannes Film Festival, held every year on the French

Riviera. A documentary on the Syrian revolution was going to be screened, and they invited me to accompany them. Thanks to their generosity, I lived many unforgettable moments in the company of movie stars, only five months after my release from prison! The trip combined business and pleasure, however; we organized several events in support of the Syrian revolution on the edges of the festival. The three days I spent in Cannes were like a fairy tale.

Back in Paris, with my appointment at OFPRA still pending and Randa and Bernard busy with their own projects, I was bored. They called me every day, but they no longer had time to meet. I started connecting to my Facebook accounts and got back in touch with friends, who were thrilled to learn I had left the West Bank and was living in Paris. A childhood friend who had fled to Belgium invited me to visit him. I accepted his offer immediately and was in Brussels the next day. We spent the week reminiscing and going to parties and barbecues. In Brussels, refugees seemed more willing to be grouped together in housing projects outside the city center. I realized how lucky I was to enjoy considerably more freedom of movement in the most beautiful city in the world.

After returning from my Belgian escapade, I learned from my father that my trial had gone ahead without the fourth witness. The military tribunal had sentenced me to seven and a half years in prison. This was the price to pay for exercising my rights to free speech and freedom of religion and for denouncing the herd mentality that held sway in my country: I would be considered a felon from now on. My father also told me that my sister Wafaa's wedding was to take place in two days and that he planned to use the occasion to announce to my family that I was now living in France. I suddenly felt sick at heart. Through the fault of the Palestinian authorities, their dictatorship and backward society, I was going to be deprived of a family celebration. I would not, as tradition holds, walk at my father's side as he accompanied my sister, and my mother would surely be saddened by my absence. I had difficulty containing my emotions but asked my father to congratulate my sister for me and to give her my best wishes.

After several gloomy days by myself, I ran into a fellow Palestinian I knew in the Métro. He introduced me to a group of his friends who were preparing a public protest to raise awareness for the Palestinian cause. Their slogans were violent, and their signs called for death to Jews and the destruction of Israel. They put out jars to collect donations. After staging an hour-long sit-in, we retreated to a brasserie to eat and count what we had taken in: almost one thousand euros, collected in hardly any time at all. The organizers were of different minds as to what to do with the money. Some wanted to divide it among everyone, while others wanted to create a community chest to help the neediest in the group. After the violent nature of their slogans, this bickering over money infuriated me, and I let them know it:

"You say you are fighting corruption in the Palestinian Authority and that you fled the country because of it. But as soon as you have some money, you use it for yourselves! You take advantage of people's suffering and the Palestinian cause to serve your own interests!"

I left before they could respond, but they were intrigued by my outburst and started asking questions. It didn't take them long to find out I was an atheist, after which they declared I was an unbeliever and cut off all ties with me.

I was unhappy living in the 18th arrondissement; it seemed so different, so far removed from the rest of the city. I noticed that there were French citizens of immigrant descent, Muslims in particular, who had not adopted democratic values and even considered these to be an affront to their own beliefs. Often, they consulted imams in their home countries on matters concerning their daily lives in France and followed their imams' advice as if it were law, in place of French legislation. This is how fatwas issued by foreign imams, which contradict French law, isolate immigrants from society at large. By following these outdated religious decrees, immigrants are inspired to revolt against the values and laws of the French republic. Those who submit to local law and order often do so out of opportunism, *taqiyah*, or the art of dissimulation.

Feeling ill at ease with my circle of acquaintances, I decided I would only associate with those friends with whom I shared the same values and the same fight and I would try to become more involved in French society.

I began to go out regularly in Paris. The city is different at night. I often met friends for drinks in brasseries, where we sometimes stayed until we were drunk, before catching the special night bus that operates after the subway shuts down. One night, a transportation officer boarded the bus to check passengers' tickets. I didn't have one. Since I couldn't pay the fine, he asked to see my papers, but when he saw my Palestinian passport, he excused himself and let me go.

That might sound like a strange reaction, but I noticed frequently that Palestine seems to occupy a special place in the French collective conscience. For the French, any Palestinian in their midst must have lost everything, endured persecution and oppression, and been in need of their help.

My social life, as much as I enjoyed it, was distracting me from my original passion: writing and publishing on the Internet. I began by creating several blogs in the style of "The Voice of Reason" but then started branching out. In one blog, I took on Salafism, using the movement's own discourse and publishing in their entirety the fatwas they had issued. To be fair, they were an easy target: Salafis had hoped to profit from the Egyptian revolution to gain traction, but the absurdity of their radicalism only turned public opinion in Egypt against them. They had made a number of bad decisions and never hid from anyone their violent and dangerous intentions.

I also published a series of articles titled, once again, "Ana Allah," telling my story and exposing the falsity of the accusations that had led to my arrest, torture, and sentencing. These got as much attention as I supposed they would: readers in Qalqilya wrote me for news of my current activities, others worried for my safety, and the rest insulted and threatened me once again. For them, my exile was all the proof they needed that I was guilty as charged: "If you had nothing to hide, you wouldn't have fled your trial, but you're a coward and your ideas are baseless and false. You preferred to run away," they said. I responded to them: "How do you expect me to stay in a place where people would like to see me dead? Didn't your Prophet flee Mecca where he was persecuted, and seek refuge in Medina? He ran away too, even though, as you believe, he had the help and support of God

Almighty. Why do you expect more from me, who stands alone against my enemies? I had no other choice."

One day, my searches on the Internet led to the official Facebook page of the Palestinian Authority, maintained by Mahmoud Abbas's own cabinet. There, I read that the President had met with the Prime Minister of Belgium about commitments made by the government to promote and protect individual freedoms in Palestine. I published a commentary on the same page, stating that there were no individual freedoms in Palestine and there was no respect for religious freedom or freedom of expression, and I told my story as an example. So many people reacted to my post that the page was taken down, and my IP address was blocked from my accessing it again.

My online activism began to attract readers. Journalists asked me to come on their shows or requested interviews or invited me to write articles. I published a long opinion piece in the *Independent*, in December 2012, which, I'm told, was read by many people and was republished by a number of media outlets. That was my first official statement since leaving the West Bank. I wanted to be clear that I was determined to pursue my fight against obscurantism, dictatorships, and despotism, and in favor of human rights and universal human values.

The holiday season was approaching, and the shop windows and streets of Paris were decorated and bright, especially the Champs-Elysées. I rang in the New Year with new friends in a new country. One year earlier, I was in the West Bank, where joy is denied its rightful place, where sadness is an occupation and hatred a passion. I decided to take advantage of the stability and generally favorable conditions that living in France had provided me to make some resolutions for 2013 and decide on some concrete next steps.

A month to the day after my column had appeared in the *Independent*, I was contacted from London by Maryam Namazie, an Iranian who is the cofounder and president of the Council of Ex-Muslims of Britain. She suggested I create a similar organization in France. She imagined that it would be linked to hers and would work in close collaboration with a

German branch. She said she was ready to come to Paris to establish the association's statutes and file the paperwork to create the association. I asked her for some time to consider her proposition; I had to be sure that the creation of a Council of Ex-Muslims of France would not interfere with my demand for political refugee status. My appointment at OFPRA had been set for January 24.

When the day finally arrived, Bernard accompanied me to OFPRA, but he was not allowed in the room during the interview. There were interpreters to translate my statements, but anyone who was not directly involved with assisting during the interview or who was not assigned to my case was asked to leave. Bernard went to have a coffee while he waited.

I found myself seated across a table from three people: my case manager, an interpreter, and a man I had never seen before. He was at pains to reassure me:

"I am the director of OFPRA. I've heard about you. I wanted to meet you and listen in on the interview. Try not to worry. Just speak frankly. You can tell us whatever you want us to know, even things you didn't have room to write in your application. Nothing you tell us will leave this room."

I tried to tell my story as objectively as possible, but I could see by the tears in their eyes that they were not unmoved by it.

When we had finished, the director of OFPRA asked me in a concerned tone:

"I read your articles on the Internet, as well as people's reactions. Do you ever stop to think that what you are doing is a death wish?"

"No, I don't, but I also didn't expect the reactions I received; not my arrest, my incarceration, or my sentencing. My beliefs ran contrary to society, and I stood up as a form of protest against everything they wanted to impose on me. It isn't suicidal to want to speak freely, improve society, and pave the way for a brighter future. On the contrary, pretending I didn't see what was happening and not fighting to create a better society, that would be preparing our collective suicide. I have no regrets, and I'm ready to continue my struggle, even knowing what the dangers are."

The director smiled warmly at me and wished me good luck. Before leaving, I confessed that I had a project but that I was waiting for OFPRA's decision on my status before going any further with it. He told me they would make a decision in the next four weeks but that he was sure the response would be positive.

I told Bernard how proud I was of that interview and how good it felt to be appreciated and to know that people wanted to help me instead of hunt me down, persecute, and threaten me. I understood then why there are no intellectuals in my country: they are either silenced, murdered, or forced into exile. Later, listening to the radio, I heard the director of OFPRA explaining the conditions necessary for political asylum status and using my own case as an example. He said he was proud to have been able to grant me asylum and that any refugee who believed in universal human values was welcome in France. I was thrilled with myself.

Now confident about the outcome of my request with OFPRA, I decided not to wait for the official announcement but to go ahead and create a Council of Ex-Muslims of France. I contacted friends and acquaintances and pulled together ten people who were ready to help prepare its opening congress.

We organized a campaign via Facebook and my blogs, asking anyone who identified with our values and agreed with our charter to join us. In just a few weeks, thirty people from all over France, but mostly from Paris, had signed on. I was notified of OFPRA's official decision in March and received a ten-year residency permit. My project to create the CEMF was already in my case file. Randa Kassis helped us, and we picked July 6, 2013, as the date of the opening congress, even though we would have liked to hold it on the symbolic date of July 1, which is the anniversary of the execution of a famous victim of religious oppression in France, Chevalier de la Barre (1766). At our first meeting, we wanted to attract attention to the threats to secularism and reassure anyone who dreamed of leaving Islam that they were not alone and that they had our full support.

A short time later, the director of the local chapter of France Terre d'Asile called me to come urgently to see him. He came right to the point:

"Now that you have a residency permit, you will have to find your own accommodation. The association can no longer be responsible for paying for your hotel room."

"But, I haven't found anywhere else to go except Saint-Denis, where an association that works with you located a room. I'm sorry, but I can't accept their offer. I wouldn't be safe there; it's as bad as living in an Islamic country: no one respects the law, radical movements impose their own laws, and the police can't even patrol there. I also have the right to stay in my room for six months after receiving my residency permit."

"I know that, but for administrative reasons, I can't let you stay. The decision has nothing to do with you personally or with religious considerations or your future projects in France. We are a nondenominational association that helps everyone, no matter their faith or ideology."

I still think this sudden revoking of my accommodation had something to do with the creation of the CEMF. He gave me a grace period of two weeks before I would have to vacate the room.

I still didn't speak French and I had already made the decision to avoid any problems or complications, so I accepted without protest. The association had helped me tremendously, and I am grateful for everything they did. I also didn't want to divert my focus from the creation of the Council.

I had two weeks to find a place to live, though I had no way of paying rent on either an apartment or a room. However, Bernard, who always had a solution, knew a friend, Aline, who owned an empty apartment in a quiet suburb of Paris. Not long after, I was settled in and could devote myself entirely to preparing the Council's opening congress. During this time, I met many Arab militants working for women's rights or freedom of religion. All of them were ex-Muslims who, for political reasons or for their safety or for social or family reasons, were discrete atheists. One of them, Atika Samrah, threw herself completely behind the project, attending public meetings, translating the proceedings, and, although it was a burden on her personal life, acting as my personal interpreter. The announcement of the creation of the CEMF attracted considerable media attention and many messages of support.

We had to be extremely vigilant: fascist and extremist parties, movements, and associations of any kind had to be prevented from infiltrating the Council and distorting our values and objectives, the better to exploit them. There was no room for error: we were walking a razor's edge.

Once the statutes were in place and the schedule of the opening congress had been decided, a few things remained to do: find a venue to host the event, make a list of attendees, and send out invitations, all before July 6.

My involvement in the Council worried my parents, but nothing could dampen their joy at the birth of Alma, my niece, whom I have never met except online. Sometimes, heartache and melancholy would get the better of me, and I would ask myself why I had to be born into such a sick society and why I wasn't like everyone else. Why did I want to rebel and make trouble for myself? Why hadn't I had a more normal life? Why did I deprive myself of so much joy with my family?

Each time I asked myself those questions, the answer came back the same: the society I knew, radicalized to the core and burdened by tribalism, has an insurmountable deficit when it comes to education, freedom, and democracy. The elites who were supposed to bring more civilized values to society deserted the cause once they became targets. One of my priorities is to give them back the role they once had and initiate a vast social reform where the influence of religion would be greatly weakened. It would be a huge undertaking.

Chapter VI
The Council of Ex-Muslims of France

We are a group of atheists. We have left Islam in the face of death threats and enormous pressure for having dared reveal our ideological and religious differences from Muslims. The backwards-looking associations and organizations of Muslims in France did not speak for us. There are even more of us than those still living in our home countries under the yoke of Islamic law are able to admit, fearing reprisals. If they are accused of apostasy and found guilty, they will be imprisoned or executed. Our goal is to desacralize Islam and encourage in its place understanding, secularism, and universal human values. We welcome all atheists, nonbelievers, areligious, secularists, intellectuals, and liberals who believe in universal values, share our commitment to secularism, defend human rights and freedoms, and are ready to work to see these principles take root all over the world.

This was the framework I used to begin my speech to the opening congress of the Council of Ex-Muslims of France (CEMF), on July 6, 2013, in Paris. I also laid out its charter, in ten points:

1. The universality of rights and equality among citizens: we oppose all forms of tolerance of inhuman beliefs; we reject all discrimination and harmful treatment practiced under the pretext of respecting a religion or a culture.
2. The freedom to criticize religion: the banning of all restrictions on the freedom of thought and speech, under any religious pretext whatsoever, and particularly in the name of the sanctity of Islam.

135

3. The freedom of religion and the freedom to be areligious and atheist.

4. The separation of Church and State: the separation of religion and education, religion, and legislation.

5. The banning of customs, habits, rules, ceremonies, or religious activities that are incompatible with peoples' rights and freedoms or that violate them.

6. The prohibition of all religious or cultural customs that infringe on the autonomy of women, penalize their freedom, and deprive them of equality. Also, the prohibition of the segregation of the sexes.

7. The prohibition of all forms of interference by any family or parental authority or by any official authority in the private lives of women and men and in their personal, emotional, and sexual relations, and in their sexuality.

8. The protection of children from all forms of manipulation and abuse by religion and by religious institutions.

9. The forbidding of all forms of financial, material, or moral supportprovided by the State or by any institution of the State to religions, their activities, and their institutions.

10. The forbidding of all forms of religious threats and intimidation.

In addition to the many people who attended the congress, others showed their support anonymously, for security reasons. Even individuals born and raised in France endure the pressure and scrutiny of their families. Others fear for their families in their home countries, some of whom may also look askance at their impiety.

The members of the Council there that day were enthusiastic, but they were especially surprised to discover the sheer number of Muslims who share their ideas and who denounce the social costs of Islam, not as a belief system, but as a way of life that regiments every last detail of their existence and interferes in the most intimate aspects of their private lives, even in a secular country like France.

The speakers congratulated the show of support for the CEMF by personalities and associations working to defend the rights of women or fighting religious fundamentalism or the Islamization of society. Some

well-known journalists were also on hand, although some tried to politicize our ideas to promote their own political agendas or extremist ideologies.

A few days after the launch of the CEMF, its Facebook page was flooded with insults and slander from Islamists but also from secularists, who, as surprising as that may seem, accused us of transplanting our problems to France. In reality, they have their heads in the sand, preferring not to look reality in the face and see the gangrenous danger posed by Islamist ghettos in France and acknowledge the complexities of the problem. A know-it-all is more dangerous than an ignoramus.

A few of our new members found that they were soon isolated by their friends and acquaintances. These "friends" were born in France and were proud of fitting into the fabric of French society, with a Western lifestyle that included drinking alcohol. Still, they couldn't tolerate any criticism of Islam. I interpret their reaction as irrefutable proof that, consciously or unconsciously, Islam infuses society and leads to the exclusion of Muslims: there are French Muslims who can defend secularism and liberalism yet reject the CEMF and fight against it.

Enough Confusion

We were satisfied with the launch of the CEMF. The congress had attracted overwhelmingly positive attention, by portraying the CEMF in the clearest possible light, which was important to ward off any attempts to exploit it politically or ideologically. The CEMF could now fulfill its role as the spokesperson for ex-Muslims and officialize their existence. Thanks to the CEMF, it is possible to be an Arab in name and ethnicity without being a Muslim, as well. Too often in the West, and in Europe particularly, the two are conflated, a pat confusion we wanted to explode. All Arabs are not Muslim; one need only think of Egyptian Copts, Lebanese Maronites, and Sudanese animists to be convinced. Likewise, not all Muslims are Arabic. In many Muslim countries (Iran, Turkey, Indonesia, Malaysia . . .), Arabs are a minority, overshadowed by other ethnic groups. Equating Arabs and Islam gives a false image of both, although Arab intellectuals living in Europe have done little to rectify that misunderstanding. The reason is self-evident: these same intellectuals never dared go public with their own departure from Islam, for fear of reprisals. This is precisely a goal of the CEMF, however: to put the growing number of atheists in touch with one another and to be their spokesperson.

It is a sad fact of history that scientists and philosophers were persecuted by Islam as heretics. Sharia law targeted intellectuals, who were hunted down and forced into exile, while their followers were executed and their books burned. Today, these same free-thinkers are put on a pedestal by Muslims, because of their contributions to the European Renaissance and their important role in Islamic civilization. Without the contributions of these writers, the history of Islam could be summed up by jihad, wars, massacres, and destruction, from the time of the Prophet to the present day.

The first person to speak up for the rights of atheists was Ismail Adham, an Egyptian intellectual who studied in Moscow and traveled in Turkey. When he returned to Egypt, he was one of the rare apostate writers to defend atheism in the Arab world. He published his famous manifesto *Why Am I an Atheist?* in Alexandria, provoking numerous reactions.

The best-known activist for the cause of atheism was Ismail Mazhar, the founder of the journal *Al-Usur*, whose motto was "Free your mind" and whose liberal ideas inspired other activists. In *Al-Usur's* introductory issue, published in 1927, Mazhar defined the journal's editorial line: science, philosophy, and literature. He defended absolute freedom of thought and expression, in all aspects of life, unburdened by the sacralization that suffocates Muslim thinkers. The courage and frank tone of *Al-Usur* contributed to its success, and many writers and journalists joined Mazar's movement: Hussein Mahmoud, who explored the ideas of Bertrand Russell, his contemporary logic, logical analysis, and analytic philosophy; Omar Annaya, who denounced "the mythological side of religion"; Jamil Sadqi al-Zahawi and Anwar Shaoul (an Iraqi Jew), who composed and published philosophical poems; and Mazhar himself, whose courageous essays against religion are particularly noteworthy. For example, he denounced the idea that God created mankind in his image, arguing instead that man imagined God in his own image. He contested, as well, the belief that God sent prophets in his name, asking:

"Why would God have chosen so many messengers in one single region that lies between the Mediterranean and the Persian Gulf? Is it because the people there helped groom the chosen ones or is it because they were living in such debauchery and obscurantism that God had no choice but to save them through the help of his prophets? But if that's true, why did God abandon everyone else? Religions are an invention little different from myths," he concluded.

Al-Usur was critical of Western writers such as Oliver Lodge, who tried to commingle science and religion through his scientific study of spiritism; Will Durant, especially his essays on Ernst Haeckel; and Frank Crane, author of *Why I Am a Christian*. Egypt's economic and financial crisis of 1931 spelled the end of *Al-Usur*, which found itself insolvent after four years, with Mazhar losing all the money he had invested in it. A Lebanese citizen, Ibrahim Haddad tried to continue the spirit of this school of free thought through a new review, *Al Duhour (The Centuries)*, but it also went bankrupt, after two years.

Though they were short-lived, these journals left their mark on Arab culture. Once they were gone, it wasn't until after the Iranian Revolution that Muslim, non-Arab intellectuals began again to take up the cause of freedom of thought: thinkers like Salman Rushdie and Ibn Warraq, among others from Iran, India, and Pakistan. The movement gained traction with the development of the Internet and social media. I may have been the first person jailed in the 21st century for daring to leave Islam and criticize it through my blogs, but many other bloggers have been arrested and persecuted in Saudi Arabia, Egypt, Tunisia, Indonesia, Bangladesh, and Iran. None of us are discouraged, however; any Internet search will quickly yield an impressive number of studies, reports, and analyses critical of Islam. The Internet will bury religion yet.

Islamophobia

Certain Muslims now use the term Islamophobia instead of speaking more clearly of anti-Arabism. This is a convenient, but completely misleading way of making it seem that Islam, specifically, is being stigmatized. Nevertheless, it is used with increasing frequency ever since the 9/11 attacks. Muslims who denounce Islamophobia display a visceral hate for everything that is not Muslim, and even for some Muslims, too: Sunnis use the term against Shiites, and vice versa. Their hatred is directed mostly at atheists and ex-Muslims, a kind of "atheist-phobia" they make no attempt to hide. One of the threats to secularism lies in the fact that Muslims can accuse anyone who opposes them of Islamophobia, with shocking ease. Such excessive recourse to this accusation does two things: on the one hand, it shows that Muslims are short on valid arguments, and, on the other, it silences secularists and atheists, who prefer to keep quiet than be accused of Islamophobia.

Rather than accept a debate on this supposed phenomenon, and advance the question by trying to make sense of it, Muslims prefer to wall themselves up in the past. They use images from the flourishing, early days of Islam to strike a tone of nostalgia with the masses and rally them around the idea of returning to a glorious past. Meanwhile, the rest of the world keeps moving forward.

However, many organizations and associations representing Muslims in France fall victim to the same backward thinking. If these associations really wanted to build a common future, uniting Muslims and non-Muslims, they wouldn't avail themselves of a supposed Islamophobia to win over naïve voters and play people off one another to their advantage.

To fight fanaticism and free Muslims from this backward-looking tendency, the media has to first stop providing a forum for the opinions of Islamist radicals, and it also has to stop relaying false accusations of Islamophobia. Meanwhile, "atheist-phobia" is growing at a dangerous pace in Islamist circles.

Politicians apply a selective secularism in the interests of political correctness. The film *Neither Allah, nor Master!* (*Ni Allah, ni Maître*) by

the Tunisian filmmaker Nadia El Fani was blocked from being screened in France, so as not to insult Muslims. The title had to be changed to *Secularism, God Willing (Laïcité Inch Allah)* before the film could be shown. Equally alarming is the silence of the French authorities on the decisions made by ulemas regarding nonbelievers; their failure to take a position equates to consent, and it is deplorable that France does not protect its Muslim residents who decide to leave Islam. The French authorities are no better than accomplices to the ulemas.

Hijab, Niqab, Burka: The Art of Manipulation

In the West, Muslims exploit Islam for political reasons. The Islamic veil (the hijab, the niqab, the burka . . .) is a good example. Nowhere in the Quran are women required to wear these, yet Muslims have seized on the veil as a way of garnering attention and creating a common, easily recognizable identity for the whole community. Moreover, this dress code makes it easier for extremist organizations to fight progressive movements and the liberalism of atheists. Not only is the veil a way of distinguishing Muslim women from European women—impious by definition—but it is also meant to send the message that Muslim women define themselves as Muslim, first and foremost. The idea is obviously nonsensical, of course, since no one defines him- or herself by religion alone. The veil is a symbol that Muslims use to impose Islam in their host countries by demanding that these countries confer certain rights on them, on their own terms.

However, the West's laxness in response to this question is a problem. Western countries have opened themselves to millions of Muslims and grant them citizenship, while they also allow these Muslim communities to live isolated in ghettos, where they demand respect for their own rules and customs before they ever dream of integrating society at large and respecting the laws of their host country. Muslims living in Great Britain are a flagrant example: they want to cast out nonbelievers, impose Ramadan (and forbid local Christians from eating in public during the entire month of fasting), prohibit the sale and consumption of alcohol, institute sharia law, and declare a jihad on Hyde Park!

French Secularism in Danger

In France, the situation is even more alarming. Simple identity checks of veiled women have degenerated into riots and acts of aggression toward police officers. These conflicts have been exploited by Islamist organizations to denounce a supposedly prevailing Islamophobia and to pressure public authorities to grant them yet more concessions.

After demanding the right to wear the niqab in public, extremists in France are now looking to obtain gender-specific hours at swimming pools, concessions for working Muslims to observe prayers, the outlawing of athletic activities for school-age girls, and a ban on male doctors from examining Muslim women. Other demands, for example, that halal meat be served in French public school cafeterias, have obvious economic motives: Islamic organizations charged with certifying the meat stand to make over 6 billion euros annually from this colossal market.

Radical movements have jumped into the cracks created by secularism and democracy and plan on using them to influence society, economics, and above all politics. They are mobilizing in ever greater numbers to enter the political scene with one, barely disguised objective: to enter the echelons of power. The consequences will surprise no one. To head off just such a regrettable evolution, France must refuse to grant any concessions and must cut off the debate, which it is far too easy to exploit. These Muslims may pretend to believe in secularism and democracy, but they also wind up becoming a threat. Secular militants, atheists, and French people throughout the country need to mobilize to defend their cultural benefits and preserve their most precious possession: secularism, the great guarantor of freedom.

Even today, too many Muslims refuse to integrate into Western society. They call for the same rights as those enjoyed by Westerners under the Universal Declaration of Human Rights, yet they refuse to recognize the responsibilities that go with it. They want to impose their religion on governments that do not recognize one and on societies who observe religion only discretely.

In France, many Muslims do not respect the government or even pay it any mind at all; their sole guide is what they hear at their mosque or from Islamic associations. On questions of marriage, divorce, education, employment, and more, a good Muslim first seeks the advice of his imam or from quranic associations, before ever turning to government services for help. Worse, some even ask radical imams in their home countries to issue fatwas against France. The many Islamic satellite television stations — Al-Manar (linked to Hezbollah), Al-Aqsa (run by Hamas), Iqra (broadcast from Saudi Arabia), Annas, and Al-Rahma (both from Egypt), to cite just a few — or sites that propose "online fatwas," threaten French secularism and help indoctrinate Muslims in France. Of course, in a global world, it is difficult to prohibit or slow the proliferation of these radical media outlets, but the most efficient way to fight these is through education, to demonstrate how the use of reason delegitimizes these imams.

Sometimes, however, and luckily, ridicule can do the job just as nicely. It's possible to read on these sites such ludicrous questions as "Will letting my beard grow increase my sexual prowess? Can a taxi refuse to drive a drunk client who is not a believer in the faith? Do women color their hair to dupe men into marrying them? Can a Muslim woman have sex while menstruating?" On television, it is also possible to hear an imam authorize a Muslim man to have sex with his wife for up to six hours after her death, or allow widowed and divorced women (but not single women, who are supposed to be virgins) to masturbate with a carrot or a cucumber.

France and the West must protect their precious secularism, if only because it is impossible for it to take hold in the Arab world.

The Fight Continues

I gave many interviews after the creation of the CEMF, but one stands out for me: an interview I granted to an Israeli media outlet that prompted violent reactions. This was to be expected; I represent a not insignificant section of Palestinian society that aspires to peace and that thinks we should work hand in hand with Israelis sharing the same vision. We have to overcome our differences and stop the violence. The same land that Palestinians want to claim as their ancestors' is also the land where many Israelis were born who have only ever known the state of Israel as their homeland. Both groups have an equal claim to the same territory and can call it home. However, the structural differences between Palestinian and Israeli society are such that it is difficult, indeed impossible, to arrive at a peaceful cohabitation between the two countries.

A peaceful solution must be found to the Israeli-Palestinian conflict. The creation of a Palestinian state will never happen, however, if people's mentalities don't change: Palestinians and Israelis both have to accept the idea of two complementary states. Similarly, there has to be an intermingling of these societies to help Palestinians catch up to modern Israelis. First, though, the hateful racism against "Jews" and "Arabs" has to be eradicated from both sides of the conflict so that they can share the same geographic space, the same workplaces, the same schools. Obviously, the need to promote secular values is a crucial step in that process.

This is the primary role of everyone who seeks peace: to move beyond traditions, customs, ideologies, and religions inherited and passed down blindly and to impose new, shared values. We must fight ideological and religious differences that divide humanity and that are the principal source of war. Given the prevailing conditions in the Middle East, it will be a long and arduous task, made even more difficult by the fact that the decision makers on both sides are extremists.

I will lead this fight hand in hand with everyone who believes in peace.

The other major battle that I have promised myself is the defense of French *laïcité* (secularism). Myself and the members of the CEMF are determined to work in concert with all French citizens who believe in secularism to protect the advances it has made in French society. Our particular role will be to help French-born Muslims to adhere to these values and to oppose anyone who tries to exploit them, as Islamists associations and organizations do.

My struggle in favor of freedom, secularism, peace, universal human rights, and, above all, the rights of women is what allows me today to enjoy a life that I have always dreamed of living, a life I imagined free of all constraints, far from the oppression of religion and its mind-dulling culture. My work in this sense makes me a better human being in that it allows me to reflect, reason, and build the future, even after the humiliations I endured and the indoctrination I refused. I defend the right to lead this revolution against my disfigured identity, my trampled humanism, my endangered existence, my travestied authenticity, my stolen dignity, and my tarnished story. I am a revolutionary, and I shoulder that role before all of humanity as I write the opening lines of my chosen life philosophy. My battle cry isn't "until victory or death," but rather "for life and humanism."

Conclusion

The society in which I was born has always fostered the dream that a writer with a frank pen would finally rewrite our somber history: a freethinker who would laugh at the speeches of tyrants and who could be bought by no one's money, no regime's promises. The society in which I was raised dreams of peace, of a world where teachers never lay a hand on their students, where girls are not murdered in the name of honor, where freedom has its place and can raise its voice, without fear of fatwas of any kind, above the retrograde values that want to stifle it.

In the twenty-first century, people dream of leaving behind the mortal, stagnant sea of religious heritage to drink from the life-giving ocean of a free society. They dream of being able to love without fearing prison, of expressing their ideas without the threat of reprisals, of a place where no despot can oppress them and where no Intelligence services can spy on their most intimate phone conversations and Internet activities. They dream of a society that outlaws the rule of religion.

The society of which I dream hopes that a new day will dawn to give life to the oldest dream in the world, handed down by mankind through the ages: FREEDOM.

So that this dream may at last come true, I declare a revolution against that dark past until my dying day. I uphold my belief in the right to dignity. I consider nothing more sacred than the freedom of the individual. My revolution has in its sights all political and religious ideologies. Its only goal is FREEDOM, whose son and soldier I am.